MINDFULNESS THAT JESUS E...

BRIAN JOHNSTON

Published by:

HAYES PRESS Publisher, Resources & Media,

The Barn, Flaxlands

Royal Wootton Bassett

Swindon, SN4 8DY

United Kingdom

www.hayespress.org

ISBN: 978-1911433569

10 9 8 7 6 5 4 3 2 1

'Merely having an open mind is nothing. The object of opening the mind, as of opening the mouth, is to shut it again on something solid.'

G.K. Chesterton

CHAPTER ONE: FILLING OUR MINDS, NOT EMPTYING THEM

After becoming the Formula 1 world motor racing champion in 2016, Nico Rosberg was asked about the secret of his success. He replied: 'I had a mental trainer and looked into meditation – actually meditation is a big word, it was more mindfulness training ... awareness.' If meditation is a big word, then mindfulness is fast becoming another one. It was virtually the word of the year in 2015. Like a rash, this word, and the idea behind it, is all over the media, being promoted as the cure-all solution to the stresses and demands of modern life. And it doesn't appear as if it's going to go away any time soon. Twenty-six schools in Cumbria in northern England have now established mindfulness as part of the school curriculum.

Educational guidelines nowadays talk a lot about supporting the emotional and mental health of pupils, and mindfulness has been the term that's been consistently trending in that connection. Its advocates claim that mindfulness isn't just a calming exercise, but rather that mindfulness, or meditation, changes the brain, creating new neural pathways and rebuilds your grey matter – in a way that reduces stress, increases happiness and heightens awareness.

Mindfulness is the trendy meditation offshoot endorsed by everyone from National Health Service departments in the United Kingdom to Oprah Winfrey in the United States. It's focused around the idea of living in the present moment, and increasing your self-awareness and curiosity. It's claimed to be life-changing. It's about how we can live well in an age dominated by technology and social pressures – which is what makes it so attractive to a great many people from top sportspersons, as we've seen, to educationalists and health practitioners. And it's an immensely attractive idea, of course. Who would not want to slow down from the frenetic pace of modern living? The pace of modern life takes its toll on our health by raising our stress levels, so who wouldn't see advantage in reducing stress by becoming more aware of our body's stress signs?

Stress is not new, of course. The Bible repeatedly shines its spotlight on the lives of people undergoing extreme stress. It does that so as to invite us to learn timeless lessons from how they coped. Take, for example, the time in good king Hezekiah's life when we read in 2 Chronicles 32:1: "After these acts of faithfulness Sennacherib king of Assyria came and invaded Judah and besieged the fortified cities, and thought to break into them for himself."

Notice the timing, 'after these acts of faithfulness.' Hezekiah had reigned for almost fourteen years, and had revived the nation's devotion to God and its temple worship, as well as having shown leadership and defeated past historic enemies of God's people. And yet, at such a time, God permitted a great test which immediately put him under extreme pressure. We can only try to imagine the stress involved when the then world superpower came knocking aggressively on his door! Thankfully, he was mindfully aware of the resource he had in God through prayer, and enlisted the prophet Isaiah's help in obtaining it. Now let's take the case of someone else under great stress, this time the prophet Elijah:

> "Now Ahab told Jezebel all that Elijah had done, and how he had killed all the prophets with the sword. Then Jezebel sent a messenger to Elijah, saying, "So may the gods do to me and even more, if I do not make your life as the life of one of them by tomorrow about this time." And he was afraid and arose and ran for his life and came to Beersheba, which belongs to Judah, and left his servant there. But he himself went a day's journey into the wilderness, and came and sat down under a juniper tree; and he requested for himself that he might die, and said, "It is enough; now, O LORD, take my life, for I am not better than my fathers" (1 Kings 19:1-4).

We read a reference there to 'all that Elijah had done.' This would include a reference to the climactic showdown Elijah had staged on Mount Carmel when he'd challenged hundreds of false prophets who'd been misleading the nation. He'd challenged them to a contest to prove whose god was the true God. It had resulted in a dramatic demonstration of the existence of the God of the prophets and founding fathers of Israel. Perhaps Elijah had especially hoped that the events on Mount Carmel would decisively turn around the top leadership in Israel. If so, Elijah forgot that people reject God despite the evidence, not because of the evidence. His death wish here, expressed so soon after his greatest victory, shows the immense strain he was under. We then have the description of what amounts to nothing short of a suicide attempt, when he left his servant behind in order to go a day's journey deeper into the unforgiving desert south of Beersheba where no-one can live for long.

Elijah wouldn't surrender to Jezebel, but he'd surrender his life to God instead. For, in depressed mood, and all burned out in service for God, and being in a state of emotional collapse, he now considered he was no better than the earlier prophets. After all, he too had failed to bring about a complete revival, hadn't he? And that even with the most spectacular of showdowns. But we could read on, if we took the time, to find out how God brings him back to the bedrock of his faith, and perhaps indicates that he was going to use Elijah in gentler ways in future. Finally, consider with me the stressful time Israel's most famous king knew:

> "Then it happened when David and his men came to Ziklag on the third day, that the Amalekites had made a raid on the Negev and on Ziklag, and had overthrown Ziklag and burned it with fire; and they took captive the women and all who were in it, both small and great, without killing anyone, and carried them off and went their way. When David and his men came to the city, behold, it was burned with fire, and their wives and their sons and their daughters had been taken captive. Then David and the people who were with him lifted their voices and wept until there was no strength in them to weep. Now David's two wives had been taken captive, Ahinoam the Jezreelitess and Abigail the widow of Nabal the Carmelite. Moreover David was greatly distressed because the people spoke of stoning him, for all the people were embittered, each one because of his sons and his daughters. But David strengthened himself in the LORD his God" (1 Samuel 30:1-6).

David was greatly distressed, as we've just read. The very word used in the text seems to hint at the pressure he was under, being a word fitted to other occasions such as when a besieged city is being described or else a cramped state of affairs. Under the pressure of so unexpected and widespread a calamity - for which he was being held personally accountable - the spirit of any other leader guided by ordinary motives would've sunk; but David, we read, encouraged himself in the LORD his God.

What's common to all these instructive examples is how the person concerned overcame by fortifying themselves with a greater awareness of God and his present help in any time of trouble (Psalm 46:1) – or more emphatically: the thought in that verse is that God can help now because he's always previously been found to have been a superlative help in past difficulties – what a stress-buster it is to be keenly aware of such a track record in any current difficulty!

But a greater sense of God can be experienced in other ways too, such as enjoying the moment whether it contains a sunset or a birdsong. Of course, the secular interest in mindfulness doesn't specifically mention God. Rather, it's about having a heightened awareness of our thoughts and feelings - for example when catching ourselves unhelpfully brooding on something; or at other times tuning into and enjoying more of what's going on around us. These would all, I think, be generally considered as being good things in themselves: the kind of things endorsed by the British National Health Service these days under the banner heading of 'mindfulness.'

While some might reject all value in such things because it smacks too much of self-absorption or maybe even because of its suspected Buddhist origins, is it not possible to trace the usefulness in the idea to a deeper root? Not to any kind of meditation which tries to empty the mind, but instead to revive the idea of biblical meditation where the mind is filled with a sense of the presence of God, the immediacy of God and his relevance to what we're experiencing at the moment. Was this not the heightened kind of awareness of God that strengthened David's hands? The Apostle Paul's Christianity was first and foremost the living out of a relationship with Jesus Christ in the here and now, in the ups and downs of everyday life. He knew how to be abased one moment and to abound the next, because in them all he, too, was aware that the Lord was strengthening him (Philippians 4:13).

As well as a balancing thoughtfulness for others, which is certainly a clear biblical emphasis, isn't it essential for our spiritual health and well-being that we sense the presence of God (e.g. see Psalm 27:4)? And isn't it important that we regularly enjoy times when we bask in our beliefs, holding scriptures in our mind, and connect more deeply with God in our lives, as we journey through each day one moment at a time? There's great merit in bringing an awareness of eternal realities into the present moment of time. I trust you agree, and in what follows, we'll try to identify 'mindfulness' in action (in this sense) in some of the great lives recounted in the Bible; and then turn from these examples to explore its value in our own lives.

CHAPTER ONE: REVIEW QUESTIONS

1. We have recalled by the help of the Bible, times of stress in the lives of Hezekiah, Elijah and David. Can you think back to a time of major stress in your life – how did you cope?

2. Psalm 46:1 is a verse that has sustained many of us at critical times in our experience. It describes God as a 'present help.' How can we become more aware of bringing the God of past help into present troubles?

3. For the Apostle Paul, God was neither historic nor remote. Which verse would you select to show the immediacy and closeness of Paul's relationship with the Lord?

4. Psalm 27:4, and its surrounding verses, invites us to reflect on true biblical meditation. What things, do you think, filled David's mind at such times as those described here? (Try to support your suggestion with biblical references.)

5. What practical steps can we take to bring an awareness of eternal realities into the present moment – and apply them beneficially to our thinking and attitude?

MAY THE MIND OF CHRIST MY SAVIOUR

May the mind of Christ my Savior, live in me from day to day,

By His love and pow'r controlling, all I do and say.

May the Word of Christ dwell richly, in my heart from hour to hour,

So that all may see I triumph, only through His pow'r.

May the peace of Christ my Savior, rule my life in every thing,

That I may be calm to comfort, sick and sorrowing.

May I run the race before me, strong and brave to face the foe,

Looking only unto Jesus, as I onward go.

May His beauty rest upon me, as I seek the lost to win,

And may they forget the channel, seeing only Him.

(Kate Barclay Wilkinson)

CHAPTER TWO: HAVING A SENSE OF GOD'S PRESENCE, POWER AND PURPOSES

We've been thinking about mindfulness as it's popularly understood in terms of becoming more intensely aware of ourselves and our surroundings and what's happening. The kind of awareness that helped Nico Rosberg by his own admission to become Formula 1 world champion in 2016. Approaching corners at two hundred miles per hour is no place for a daydreamer, preoccupied with anything other than negotiating the rapidly approaching bend! But returning to the more serious demands of life, we want to explore if there's any sense in which being more aware of the true state of reality at each moment is something that the Bible would endorse. And we're building up to what the Lord Jesus had to say on this. With that goal in mind, let's set about trying to identify what could reasonably be called 'mindfulness' in great Bible lives. We'll visit first the camp of Israel with the young shepherd boy, David – on the day he became famous in Israel. It was a time of war.

> "Now the Philistines gathered their armies for battle; and they were gathered at Socoh which belongs to Judah, and they camped between Socoh and Azekah, in Ephes-dammim.

Saul and the men of Israel were gathered and camped in the valley of Elah, and drew up in battle array to encounter the Philistines. The Philistines stood on the mountain on one side while Israel stood on the mountain on the other side, with the valley between them. Then a champion came out from the armies of the Philistines named Goliath, from Gath, whose height was six cubits and a span. He had a bronze helmet on his head, and he was clothed with scale-armor which weighed five thousand shekels of bronze. He also had bronze greaves on his legs and a bronze javelin slung between his shoulders. The shaft of his spear was like a weaver's beam, and the head of his spear weighed six hundred shekels of iron; his shield-carrier also walked before him. He stood and shouted to the ranks of Israel and said to them, "Why do you come out to draw up in battle array? Am I not the Philistine and you servants of Saul? Choose a man for yourselves and let him come down to me" (1 Samuel 17:1-8).

Picture an encampment with two armies facing off against each other. From the perspective of the people known in the Old Testament as the people of God, Israel, they watch as out of the enemy camp facing them strides a nine-foot giant of a man. He describes Israel as the servants of Saul and defies them to produce a worthy opponent for him to face in single mortal combat. This was his proposal for how the outcome of the war might be decided. It's easy to sense the reaction of those cowering before the giant. All the men of Israel saw the man coming up to defy Israel and it says: "When all the men of Israel saw the man, they fled from him and were greatly afraid" (1 Samuel 17:24).

Naturally, their attention was fixed on this challenger who was defying Israel and taunting them as the servants of Saul. They were truly, it seems, no more mindful of who they were than to acknowledge they were the servants of Saul, and facing a formidable challenge. The teenager, David, had come among the Israelite army to visit his older brothers who were serving soldiers. He saw what they saw. But he saw more. Much more. And what he was aware of in addition, would determine the outcome of that day. Listen: "Then David spoke to the men who were standing by him, saying, "What will be done for the man who kills this Philistine and takes away the reproach from Israel? For who is this uncircumcised Philistine, that he should taunt the armies of the living God?" (1 Samuel 17:24-26).

I don't detect fear or even dismay in that question, do you? To the young David this wasn't a huge intimidating challenger to be afraid of – he was a mere uncircumcised Philistine enemy soldier. What's more, it was the giant who was in mortal danger for he'd not taunted the servants of Saul, but in reality he'd taunted the armies of the living God! Even a nine-foot, fully armed warrior has no chance against the omnipotent creator! David was completely aware of all this. A sense of the living God permeated his entire existence. And that changed everything – for he remembered well how God had helped him defend his father's flock of sheep from the threat of a lion and a bear. David became champion in the Vale of Elah that day because of his awareness of God as a present reality in any danger he faced. He was not alone. For David, it was always going to be a one-sided contest – but not in the way the rest of the army viewed it! We face giants of different sorts. Huge obstacles and challenges at times confront us. They dismay us, but are we aware that we're not alone? It's good to explore the lesson David's example teaches us in our own lives.

But let's come now to the New Testament, and the greatest example. It's quite likely, we believe, that the room in which the Lord Jesus gave his final instructions to His disciples before he went out to die on the cross was a room with a view. It's certainly possible, if not probable, that it gave a view out over Jerusalem and its surrounding valleys. But what was the outlook of the man who was gathering his followers for that last supper?

For him, the cross was now sharply in view. But there was a still greater awareness, as we soon discover:

> "Now before the Feast of the Passover, Jesus knowing that His hour had come that He would depart out of this world to the Father, having loved His own who were in the world, He loved them to the end. During supper, the devil having already put into the heart of Judas Iscariot, the son of Simon, to betray Him, Jesus, knowing that the Father had given all things into His hands, and that He had come forth from God and was going back to God, got up from supper and laid aside His garments; and taking a towel, He girded Himself ... and began to wash the disciples' feet" (John 13:1-5).

This was certainly pre-meditated action. Knowing his hour had come, he rose from supper – and bent down to wash the dusty feet of his twelve proud disciples – none of whom had been prepared to perform such a menial task for the others in the group. They were vying with each other for greatness, so the Lord himself had to take the lowest place to teach them a lesson in humility they never forgot. What presence of mind – just hours before his shameful death! Christians to this day are moved to consider the Lord dramatizing in that way the greater condescension that was in progress by which he, as the Lord of glory, had laid aside that glory and stepped down to earth, down to the depthless abasement of the cross. "Knowing the Father had given all things into his hands ...", what an acute awareness of the significance of the moment in terms of his destiny!

What about us? What should we as Christians be constantly mindful of at every moment? Romans chapter 6 and Colossians chapter 3 would be excellent Bible chapters to hide in our heart and hold in our minds. That could only help foster in us an awareness that our Christian life's true perspective is lived out from an awareness of our union with Christ. Those chapters are full of it, and the practical consequences that follow from it. We'll come to explore them later, but for now, our closing reflection is on Romans chapter 8 with its five unanswerable questions:

"If God is for us, who is against us? He who did not spare His own Son, but delivered Him over for us all, how will He not also with Him freely give us all things? Who will bring a charge against God's elect? God is the one who justifies; who is the one who condemns? Christ Jesus is He who died, yes, rather who was raised, who is at the right hand of God, who also intercedes for us. Who will separate us from the love of Christ?" (Romans 8:31-35).

It's got to be healthy for us to keep these unanswerable questions in our mind at every moment of our lives!

CHAPTER TWO: REVIEW QUESTIONS

1. What do you think enabled David to see more than the others saw?
2. David regarded the army not so much as Saul's army, but as the army of the living God. How can we apply the same refocusing to our money, talents, family, job etc?
3. Every action of our Lord in his earthly life had the cross as its reference point. How can we adopt a similar mindset with the Lord's return as our reference point?
4. In what way does mindfulness of the 5 highlighted questions from the end of Romans 8 help us to overcome momentary feelings of defeatism, pessimism, etc.?

LORD JESUS, TEACH US STILL TO KEEP

Lord Jesus, teach us still to keep

Our eyes on You, the Living Way

That we, once lost and wandering sheep,

From You, O Lord, no more may stray;

But wherever you lead we

May follow on most cheerfully.

Oh, that we never might forget

What You have suffered for our sake,

To save our souls and make us fit,

In all Thy glory to partake;

But keeping this in sight, press on

To glory and a victor's crown.

(James Deck)

CHAPTER THREE: BEING MINDFUL OF THE THINGS OF GOD

We talk about someone going from 'hero to zero'. I think we could say that more than once about the Apostle Peter whenever we think about his interactions with Jesus, as we have them reported in the Gospels. Being often the first one to speak, meant that he seemed to get it wrong as often as he got it right. Take, for example, the time ...

"... when Jesus came into the district of Caesarea Philippi, He was asking His disciples, "Who do people say that the Son of Man is?" And they said, "Some say John the Baptist; and others, Elijah; but still others, Jeremiah, or one of the prophets." He said to them, "But who do you say that I am?" Simon Peter answered, "You are the Christ, the Son of the living God." And Jesus said to him, "Blessed are you, Simon Barjona, because flesh and blood did not reveal this to you, but My Father who is in heaven. "I also say to you that you are Peter, and upon this rock I will build My church; and the gates of Hades will not overpower it. "I will give you the keys of the kingdom of heaven; and whatever you bind on earth shall have been bound in heaven, and whatever you loose on earth shall have been loosed in heaven." Then He warned the disciples that they should tell no one that He was the Christ.

From that time Jesus began to show His disciples that He must go to Jerusalem, and suffer many things from the elders and chief priests and scribes, and be killed, and be raised up on the third day. Peter took Him aside and began to rebuke Him, saying, "God forbid it, Lord! This shall never happen to You." But He turned and said to Peter, "Get behind Me, Satan! You are a stumbling block to Me; for you are not setting your mind on God's interests, but man's." Then Jesus said to His disciples, "If anyone wishes to come after Me, he must deny himself, and take up his cross and follow Me. For whoever wishes to save his life will lose it; but whoever loses his life for My sake will find it" (Matthew 16:13-25).

There's a lot we can learn from that exchange: for example, how at first Peter got it right, speaking by revelation about Jesus' true identity; but then how quickly he went from hero to zero, as it were, by saying quite inappropriately that the Lord wouldn't die on the cross. That brings us to the Lord's critique of Peter when he replied: "Get behind Me, Satan! You are an offense to Me, for you are not mindful of the things of God, but the things of men" (NKJV).

'You are not mindful of the things of God' - how often might that criticism be addressed to us? That's important for us to consider when we're thinking about this idea of mindfulness which has become fashionable in recent years, at least in some parts of the world. Mindfulness is a kind of meditation: one that aims to heighten awareness. Every Christian must surely want a greater sense of God in his or her life. Mindfulness can be excellent, depending on what it is we're being mindful of. Mindfulness of the things of God would have prevented Peter from being Satan's agent in this instance. Can we not conclude from Jesus' words here, that being mindful of God's things should be our aim at all times? Central to God's interests is the cross of Christ. That much is made clear in the first chapter of First Corinthians:

> "For the word of the cross is foolishness to those who are perishing, but to us who are being saved it is the power of God. For it is written, "I WILL DESTROY THE WISDOM OF THE WISE, AND THE CLEVERNESS OF THE CLEVER I WILL SET ASIDE." Where is the wise man? Where is the scribe? Where is the debater of this age? Has not God made foolish the wisdom of the world? For since in the wisdom of God the world through its wisdom did not come to know God, God was well-pleased through the foolishness of the message preached to save those who believe. For indeed Jews ask for signs and Greeks search for wisdom; but we preach Christ crucified, to Jews a stumbling block and to Gentiles foolishness, but to those who are the called, both Jews and Greeks, Christ the power of God and the wisdom of God. Because the foolishness of God is wiser than men, and the weakness of God is stronger than men" (1 Corinthians 1:18-25).

The Apostle Paul, guided by the Spirit, began there by quoting from the prophet Isaiah. It was back in the 29th chapter of Isaiah that God had forewarned that he was one day going to do something 'wondrously marvellous' which would utterly confound human wisdom. God fulfilled that promise in the most wonderful and marvellous way possible at the cross. Philosophers ('wise men') ever since have struggled to fit the cross into their ways of viewing the world; religious traditionalists ('scribes') don't consider it to be at all the kind of sign they'd expect; and the professional debaters who were around in the first century doubtless found it a topic quite unsuited for their art.

Not much has changed since. Contemporary intellectuals dismiss what they view as the sadistic and horrific barbarism of the cross. They hold in utter contempt any god who could conceive of such a deed as the Bible claims occurred at the cross. They do this in a similar vein to what's shown in an early piece of graffiti where Christians and their God were the butt of the joke. It displays a figure on a cross with a donkey's head, and under the man drawn beside it, the inscription reads, 'Alexander worships his god.' Recently, Stephen Fry (the UK TV presenter) was threatened with a blasphemy charge for broadcast views in the south of Ireland, in which he railed at the stupidity of a god in making a world full of injustice. Outspoken atheist, Richard Dawkins, likewise slanders the bloodthirstiness of a genocidal god whom he calls 'the most unpleasant character in all of fiction' – and then states it gets even worse in the New Testament because in his view that was basically 'cosmic child abuse.' The latter may be another's phrase (Steve Chalke), but doubtless Dawkins would fully support it. What all these excerpts show is how the cross is viewed by intellectuals today as utter foolishness. They hold it in contempt. In that, the world in its wisdom is on display, and God has destroyed their wisdom.

If we're to be mindful of the things of God, then we'll have the highest view of God's purpose at the cross. We learn that from the Lord's rebuke of Peter. The hymn-writer says it well:

'Jesus, keep me near the cross

Bring its scenes before me

Let me live from day to day

With its shadow o'er me.'

The hour of our Lord's death was always on his mind, he was at all times aware that his destiny lay there. It should always draw our thoughts too. At another time, he famously said: 'Seek first God's kingdom and his righteousness, and all these things will be added to you' (Mathew 6:33). Being mindful of the things of God, as a priority concern, is basic to our relationship with the Lord. And since Christianity is all about that relationship, this is a big deal. After all, this is what sets Christianity apart from all of the world's religions, since at its core it's about our personal relationship with its founder. The Apostle Paul captured the very essence of the Christian life when he said that his desire was that he might know him (Philippians 3:10). Paul was a mentor for Timothy, and because he also wanted Timothy to grow in his true experience of Christ, he said this to him: "Meditate upon these things ... immerse yourself in them, so that all may see your progress" (1 Timothy 4:15 ESV).

He was referring to Timothy's conduct, his Bible-reading, teaching ministry and spiritual giftedness. Those were the things he was to meditate on and immerse himself in. It's probably worth a more detailed look at these. Let's reverse back up the chapter. From verse 7, Paul says:

> "Train yourself for godliness; for while bodily training is of some value, godliness is of value in every way, as it holds promise for the present life and also for the life to come. The saying is trustworthy and deserving of full acceptance. For to this end we toil and strive, because we have our hope set on the living God, who is the Savior of all people, especially of those who believe. Command and teach these things. Let no one despise you for your youth, but set the believers an example in speech, in conduct, in love, in faith, in purity. Until I come, devote yourself to the public reading of Scripture, to exhortation, to teaching. Do not neglect the gift you have, which was given you by prophecy when the council of elders laid their hands on you. Practice these things, immerse yourself in them, so that all may see your progress. Keep a close watch on yourself and on the teaching. Persist in this, for by so doing you will save both yourself and your hearers" (1 Timothy 4:7-16).

Timothy was to set an example for others in the way he spoke, in the way he acted – in fact, he was to be a role model for other believers in the demonstration of his love, and his faith, and his purity. He was to set the tone for others by reading and sharing the Bible and its teaching. In doing so, he'd be operating out of his spiritual gifting from God. These were the practical disciplines by means of which Timothy would remain mindful of the things of God. And the same remains true for us.

CHAPTER THREE: REVIEW QUESTIONS

1. From the dialogue between Peter and the Lord, sketch in as much detail as you can what mindfulness of God's things might look like.
2. Try to shortlist a few favourite hymns that are meditative upon the cross of Christ. What benefit do you gain from having this same mindset?
3. The Apostle Paul gives Timothy a checklist of things to meditate upon. Which, from that list, do you find to be the most challenging?
4. Any helpful suggestions regarding some of the others?
5. What does being mindful of God's kingdom and righteousness involve in practice?

FILL THOU MY LIFE, O LORD MY GOD

Fill Thou my life, O Lord my God, in every part with praise,

That my whole being may proclaim, Thy being and Thy ways.

Not for the lip of praise alone, nor e'en the praising heart,

I ask, but for a life made up, of praise in every part.

Praise in the common things of life, its goings out and in;

Praise in each duty and each deed, however small and mean.

So shall each fear, each fret, each care, be turned into song

And every winding of the way, the echo shall prolong.

So shall no part of day or night, from sacredness be free,

But all my life, in every step, be fellowship with Thee.

(H. Bonar)

CHAPTER FOUR: RENEWING YOUR MIND

We all have things we desire. Whether or not that's wrong depends on what it is that we desire. After the original sin, the consequence for all of us was that we lost the ability to desire God. The Apostle Peter, writing to Christian believers, encourages them to live the rest of their time ... no longer for the lusts of men, but for the will of God (1 Peter 4:2). The lusts of men don't – and can't - express any desire for God. Our motivations are bound up with our desires, and yet we can influence them. Spiritual disciplines can shape our habits. But how exactly can our desires, motivations and habits be reformed? How does the process work?

When the Spirit of God communicates with the spirit of our mind, he uses God's Word, bringing it to our attention. The Word of God is the instrument of revival. But why is there sometimes revival without reformation – at either a personal or national level? To take an example, in the 1980s, a Gallup poll survey in the US returned the result that a very high percentage of people believed the Bible to be God's Word. But alongside that, the poll also found that there was no discernible difference between Christians and non-Christians when it came down to deciding upon moral and ethical issues. In other words, Christianity was making a vanishingly small impact on the surrounding culture.

By way of contrast, in eighteenth-century England, the Wesleyan revival produced a nationwide reformation that has even been recognized by secular historians – historians who said that it had spared England the fate that had befallen the French – that is, England had escaped a Revolution. Before England's eighteenth-century Revival - prior to England being impacted by God's Word - it was a land of drugs, drunks and bloodsports. By contrast, for all the estimated 60 million Christian believers that were estimated to be in the US in the 1980s, it appears that the spirit of the age, and a focus on worldly media, had shaped the thought patterns of believers - such that revival - if we can even call it that - had not then, nor now, produced any noticeable reformation of behaviour. Why the difference between America's experience in the twentieth century and that of England in the eighteenth century? The missing element in modern times in the western world has been a failure to pay personal attention to spiritual transformation.

That's a rather big statement, and we're going to have to explain what we mean by 'spiritual transformation.' Let's get into that now. The Apostle Paul, for only the second time in his letter to Christians at Rome, issues commands or imperatives in the twelfth chapter when he says: "Don't be conformed to this world, but be transformed by the renewing of your mind, so that you may prove what the will of God is, that which is good and acceptable and perfect" (Romans 12:2). Notice that he mentions the renewing of the mind. That's how transformation comes about; that's how change can be effected. Habits and behaviours will never be changed unless we have our thinking renewed. As Paul says, our mind has to be renewed. The passive alternative is to have our thinking shaped by the influence of the world around us - namely by the pressure of our peers, as (for example) when we instinctively and brainlessly like what others are liking on Facebook.

The world is so good at squeezing us into its mould in the same way jelly takes the shape of whatever mould you choose to put it into when you pour it out as liquid and let it set. When instead we allow our perceptions to be adjusted by what we read in God's Word, our minds are renewed, and this biblical kind of transformation takes place. Which mould for our thinking will we choose? Will it be an ungodly world or God's Word? Beware of an untransformed mind. It's such a poor Christian testimony. Transformation is exactly what happens to the caterpillar as it morphs into a butterfly. It's also the same word - as used biblically - for the transfiguration of the Lord's natural body in Matthew 17. You remember how we're told that he was then glorified in it, as he will also be in his mystical body, the Church. But that lies in the future. We want to remain in the present, where in practical terms, being renewed to a proper mindfulness of God means affirming that God's will is best (Rom.12:2). That way we'll escape the censure Peter received when failing to discern God's will. He foolishly attempted to deflect the Lord's purpose away from the cross. That was when he received the rebuke that he was not being mindful of the things of God. Other things, worldly ambitions, were uppermost in his mind then, displacing God's plans.

Now, when we come to Second Corinthians chapter 4, we hear the Apostle Paul speaking out of personal experience – he speaks there about: "Carrying about in the body the dying of Jesus ... our outer man is decaying, yet our inner man is being renewed day by day. For momentary, light affliction is producing for us an eternal weight of glory far beyond all comparison" (2 Corinthians 4:10,16,17). Notice this also mentions an inner renewal, and gives us another angle on it. The context here is Paul talking very candidly to the Corinthians about some of his many afflictions in service for the Lord. His theme teaches that blessings come out of buffetings. As well as the spreading of grace through the progress of the Gospel as it's preached, inner renewal takes place in the Lord's servant - the Christian worker - who as a result of mistreatment has the opportunity of becoming like Jesus in his death ('the dying of Jesus'). If you're facing difficulties even as you try to live faithfully for the Lord, allow yourself to feel encouragement from Paul's words. In the longer term, in the bigger picture of our lives, there's no comparison between present frustrations and future glories.

As we continue our biblical exploration of spiritual transformation through this biblical renewal process, we next come to Paul's teaching to the church at Colossae. In chapter 3, he says: "You have been raised up with Christ, keep seeking the things above, where Christ is, seated at the right hand of God. Set your mind on the things above ... and ... put on the new self who is being renewed to a true knowledge according to the image of the One who created him" (Colossians 3:1,2,10). Renewal again, you'll note. This is the right way in which to be other-worldly or heavenly-minded. When we're heavenly-minded in this way, then we are of maximum earthly use for the Lord. It's about living at a higher level – and so not falling short of God's image through behaving in ways inconsistent with our new identity as a Christian.

This Bible text is about the sort of mindfulness that's produced in a believer on the Lord Jesus when he or she is moment by moment practising what it means to be conscious of eternal realities. We've just spoken about living at a higher level through this kind of mindfulness. I want now to give you an illustration of that. In an earlier age of flying, a man was in an old biplane, a very flimsy and primitive machine compared to what we're now used to. As he flew it solo, complete with helmet and goggles in the open cockpit, he heard with some alarm a gnawing sound. Very soon, he realized this meant there was a rat on board – a little stowaway that was at that moment endangering his life! What if that sound was it chewing its way through something vital – a fuel line perhaps? There was no time to reach land safely, so the pilot did the opposite. He flew higher and higher! As the little plane progressively gained altitude, the gnawing sound stopped. In the higher air, there was less oxygen and the rat couldn't survive. He was now safe! The things that endanger our spiritual lives can become dormant if we live at a higher level by setting our mind on things above, consistent with the rule of Christ.

In this famous Bible section of Colossians 3:1-17, we're taught how to ensure our conflicted desires and motives (vv.12-14) are arbitrated by the peace of Christ. It happens when we allow his Word to reside in us for our instruction and admonition. By opening our spirit to his, to receive his revelation in the Word, it engages our mind, and filters down to our heart, there it shapes our will, and sets the course of our whole life. In all of this, mindfulness is the key. If we're constantly mindful of our having died with Christ, and of the present status of our life as 'hidden with Christ in God,' we'll discover the motivation to put to death, by the Spirit, the deeds of our body: meaning things like immorality and greed.

A previous generation of Christians called this process 'mortification.' Day by day, as we journey to that destiny, we should be actively concerned to exchange the elements of self for those of his character, namely compassion, kindness, humility, gentleness, patience, forgiveness, love. It's mindfulness of our union with Christ that motivates the discipline of endeavouring that our every action should be characteristic of the Lord. But Paul's not yet done talking on this practical topic of spiritual renewal of our mind. In Ephesians chapter 4, he says:

> "Walk no longer just as the Gentiles ... in the futility of their mind, being darkened in their understanding, excluded from the life of God ... because of the hardness of their heart ... have given themselves over to sensuality ... But you did not learn Christ in this way ... in reference to your former manner of life ... lay aside the old self ... be renewed in the spirit of your mind, and put on the new self, which ... in the likeness of God ... has

been created in righteousness and holiness of the truth" (Ephesians 4:17-24).

Here, finally, it's explicitly the renewal of the spirit of our mind. It's about forsaking a lifestyle of futility by learning of Christ. It's about Christ becoming everything to us (Colossians 3:11). After a performance of Beethoven's Ninth Symphony, the audience gave conductor ArturoToscanini and the Philadelphia Philharmonic Orchestra a prolonged ovation. Toscanini, turned to his musicians and whispered, "Gentlemen," You are nothing," he said. That didn't surprise them apparently, since his routine method for extracting more performance from them was to belittle or criticize their play. But what he said next did shock them, for he said: "And I am nothing." Then he added, "But Beethoven is everything!" Our aim is to get to the point in Christian experience when we can truly say 'I am nothing, but Christ is everything.' He must increase and we must decrease.

To get there, we've to lay aside – we've to forsake – past futile ways. That's the first step before we can put on - before we can learn - Christ. Personal spiritual transformation is about exchanging elements of our corrupted self for the elements of his character by renewing the spirit of our mind. This is clear in the text that talks about laying aside the futile elements and then putting on the new self, as renewed in the image of God. This is still all by God's grace, of course, but it does still require effort on our part. Grace is opposed to earning, but not to effort. Indeed, spiritual fitness takes a whole lot of effort. By the renewing of our mind comes the reforming of our character, one behaviour or one habit at a time.

CHAPTER FOUR: REVIEW QUESTIONS

1. Every action begins as a thought. Which is it more effective to try to modify?
2. Self-awareness is a vital first step to change. Make a list of some of the ways in which the world tries to shape our lives.
3. The decay of our 'outer man' is inevitable. Inner renewal is not. How can we foster it?
4. What do you think is the key idea shared in Col.3:1-17? (Hint: what is it that facilitates our mindfulness being on 'higher things'?)
5. What is the biblical prescription for reforming our lives one (character) element at a time?

LOVED WITH EVERLASTING LOVE

Loved with everlasting love,

Led by grace that love to know;

Spirit, breathing from above,

You have taught me it is so.

Oh, this full and perfect peace!

Oh, this transport all divine!

In a love which cannot cease,

I am His, and He is mine.

Heaven above is softer blue,

Earth around is sweeter green;

Something lives in every hue

Christless eyes have never seen:

Birds with gladder songs o'erflow,

Flow'rs with deeper beauties shine,

Since I know, as now I know,

I am His, and He is mine.

(G.W. Robinson)

CHAPTER FIVE: CHANGING YOUR MIND (AND YOUR LIFE) IN FOUR 'Rs'

From one of the words used in it, the Jews call the following the ancient 'Shema' (Deuteronomy 6:4-9; where the last letter of the first word in this verse, 'Shema,' means 'hear'):

> "Hear, O Israel! The LORD is our God, the LORD is one! You shall love the LORD your God with all your heart and with all your soul and with all your might. These words, which I am commanding you today, shall be on your heart. You shall teach them diligently to your sons and shall talk of them when you sit in your house and when you walk by the way and when you lie down and when you rise up. You shall bind them as a sign on your hand and they shall be as frontals on your forehead. You shall write them on the doorposts of your house and on your gates."

Jews read it at least twice a day, morning and evening. What this illustrates is the mindset, the focus, which they have long placed on Scripture memorization. We can learn from that. We need to think correctly and often about God, if we want to live like Christ. We've been emphasising that what shapes our character and way of life is what our mind concentrates on, and what ends up going down to the heart. This is the value of a daily routine featuring meditation on God's Word. And I'd include actual Scripture memorisation in that. Probably nothing can promote the true value of mindfulness in our lives more than this daily discipline.

But you might say 'I don't have a good memory.' What you probably mean is you don't have a trained memory. What's the cure for an untrained memory? **C**oncentration, **U**nderstanding, and **R**epetition. Some people can commit to memory large portions of the Bible. There's value in that, of course, but we're not talking here about any kind of performance or competition. Perhaps the greatest value is to focus on strategic paragraphs of God's Word and absorb them, internalize them, allowing the truths they contain to fill our minds as we wake and go to sleep, as well as occupying our mind with it at suitable moments during the day.

May I suggest a really helpful section to attempt this with is Colossians chapter three and the first seventeen verses. Those verses begin with the very point we're considering – that of focusing our mind on right things – in other words of being mindful of the very truth that will elevate our living. And for the remainder they're themed on moving on from this focus to bring about real change in our lives. Let's read that section now:

> "Therefore if you have been raised up with Christ, keep seeking the things above, where Christ is, seated at the right hand of God. Set your mind on the things above, not on the things that are on earth. For you have died and your life is hidden with Christ in God. When Christ, who is our life, is revealed, then you also will be revealed with Him in glory. Therefore consider the members of your earthly body as dead to immorality, impurity, passion, evil desire, and greed, which amounts to idolatry.

For it is because of these things that the wrath of God will come upon the sons of disobedience, and in them you also once walked, when you were living in them. But now you also, put them all aside: anger, wrath, malice, slander, and abusive speech from your mouth. Do not lie to one another, since you laid aside the old self with its evil practices, and have put on the new self who is being renewed to a true knowledge according to the image of the One who created him - a renewal in which there is no distinction between Greek and Jew, circumcised and uncircumcised, barbarian, Scythian, slave and freeman, but Christ is all, and in all.

So, as those who have been chosen of God, holy and beloved, put on a heart of compassion, kindness, humility, gentleness and patience; bearing with one another, and forgiving each other, whoever has a complaint against anyone; just as the Lord forgave you, so also should you. Beyond all these things put on love, which is the perfect bond of unity. Let the peace of Christ rule in your hearts, to which indeed you were called in one body; and be thankful. Let the word of Christ richly dwell within you, with all wisdom teaching and admonishing one another with psalms and hymns and spiritual songs, singing with thankfulness in your hearts to God. Whatever you do in word or deed, do all in the name of the Lord Jesus, giving thanks through Him to God the Father" (Colossians 3:1-17).

Time and again, the Apostle Paul taught that the definition of being a Christian believer is that we've in fact died – that is, we're precisely those who have died with Christ. And he does it again here – "you died ... with Christ." There can hardly be any reality more foundational to appropriate Christian living than this. And the early part of Colossians 3 starts off with that: with our true and new identity, who we really are. We're those who are in union with Christ. That has to be something we're daily mindful of if we're going to live well as a Christian. This is about taking the invisible – lives hidden with Christ in God – and making them into a visible reality before others. Our lives are hidden with Christ in God, but our daily lifestyle should be making this obvious to other people living in close proximity to us. There should be no such thing as a nominal Christian, in a sense that's a contradiction in terms. We're meant to be transformational Christians.

And this seventeen-verse paragraph from God's Word gives us the recipe. It's all about transformation. It talks about laying aside the old, and putting on the new in terms of habitual behaviours. There's habit-forming discipline involved in changing from a being a nasty, impatient person into becoming a person characterized by kindness and patience. This same section of the Bible will come to that. But – and this is something we need to be absolutely convinced about – behaviour modification begins with the mind. Effort alone will not be successful, our mind must direct that effort. I don't think any counsellor would dispute that – but this is not coming from the pages of any counselling manual, but from the very Word of God, the God who made us, and who understands infinitely better than we do how we work.

I'm old enough to have learned 'the 3Rs' at school. If ever there was a misnomer, that was it. It doesn't exactly encourage accurate spelling and good pronunciation because only one of the three represented words actually begin with the letter 'r', but it did still serve an educative purpose. I'm going to suggest we replace that in the Christian school of life with 'the 4Rs' and this time they represent 4 words that actually do all begin with the letter 'r' as properly spoken! I want us to remember: 'Revelation, Revival, Renewal, and Reformation' – and come to understand how they fit together in that order in a potentially life-changing sequence.

It's not automatic, of course; very few things worth having are. And we will additionally identify the appropriate Christian disciplines needed to develop Christlikeness. It does boil down to breaking bad habits and making good habits. But it's a strategy directed by our mind – and what's most important of all – by a mind illuminated by biblical truth that's correctly understood as life-changing. This is no twisting of scripture to support some kind of psychological theory, it's about explaining and directly applying foundational Christian truths about how God intends that we live.

As we put it together, I want you to be able to see that it's a simple set of steps. What's more, each step is a do-able step. Together we'll see, how the revelation of God's Word – through memorization and other disciplines involving our Spirit, Mind, Heart and Soul – all combine to reform our character. So, it begins with **revelation**. God communicates with our spirit. By understanding and absorbing that communication, helped in part by memorising it, we allow it to **revive** us. We set our mind on the truths we've read. Having become intent on God's Word in that way, our mind becomes **renewed**, which in turn allows its truth to penetrate down into our heart. Since our heart sets our purpose, the outcomes of our life will be influenced. In other words, our decisions, then our habits, and finally our character undergoes **reformation**.

If you like, we could label this the S.I.M.P.L.E.S.T. method where the letters of 'simplest' stand for reminders of the sequence that starts with our Spirit, moves to focus on the Intent of the Mind, leading to Penetration down through the heart into our LifE, with the end result being that the life of our Soul becomes Transformed. The initial letters of these key words spell out the acronym SIMPLEST. This is what we are calling a method to be explained in detail later ...

CHAPTER FIVE: REVIEW QUESTIONS

1. What do you consider to be the biggest disincentive to Scripture memorization?

2. Does it help to overcome that if we were to understand such memorization as being a real help to the kind of mindfulness we're exploring biblically? What do you see as its particular value?

3. We are suggesting that we should memorize Col.3:1-17. Why, in particular, do you think this passage has been selected?

4. What would you say is the basic idea that this text presents us with - one that is key to understanding our new Christian identity?

A MIND AT PERFECT PEACE WITH GOD

A mind at perfect peace with God;

O what a word is this!

A sinner reconciled through blood;

This, this indeed is peace.

By nature and by practice far,

How very far from God;

Yet now by grace brought nigh to Him,

Through faith in Jesus' blood.

So nigh, so very nigh to God,

I cannot nearer be;

For in the person of His Son

I am as near as He.

Why should I ever anxious be,

Since such a God is mine?

He watches o'er me night and day,

And tells me "Mine is thine."

(C. Paget)

CHAPTER SIX: PUTTING OFF – THE FORGOTTEN BIBLICAL DISCIPLINE OF MORTIFICATION

We've already been thinking of God's work in us. It being his will to work for his good pleasure in our life – and that's very simply expressed as the formation in us of a resemblance to Christ – so that we should bear a family resemblance to his son. Simple to express it may be, but it's not easy to overcome the various forms of opposition which God's enemy orchestrates against us to frustrate this epic purpose of God in our Christian lives. God's enemy is also our enemy.

Let's return to our 4 Rs which we've defined as being: Revelation; Revival; Renewal; and Reformation. Taking the first R of Revelation, we understand from the Bible itself (Romans 8:16) that God communicates with our human spirit, and normally this takes place as we read in his Word, the Bible. As God's Word engages with our mind, the stage is set for Revival, the second R in our sequence. But will this revival bring about the end result of the personal reformation of our character? For this work of God to progress in us, we'll need to be intentional. It's another reading of Colossians 3:2 which literally speaks of the intent of our mind. Do we skim-read God's Word? Or are we intent on what we read? Intentional reading of God's Word – which is where we absorb and internalize its truth content - is intensified if through the spiritual disciplines of meditation and memorization, we intentionally set our minds on the truth contained in our Bible reading. In this way, our mind is set for renewal, which is the gradual readjustment of our thought patterns.

We've now picked up our third R, for Renewal. This world's messages, which constantly bombard us through the media, affect our thinking far more than we care to realize. Have you ever encountered a believer rejecting a plain interpretation of a Bible text as being grossly unfair? Chances are, that's the thinking of a worldly believer, reflecting the value system of the age in which we live. We can all do that, at times. The world's values, and what it considers to be fair, are often so different from the Bible's. The only antidote is to be constantly allowing biblical truth to penetrate down into our heart where it shapes our will and leads to the reforming of our soul, being our fourth and final R – which stands for Reformation, or in other words, the transformation of our spiritual life. It's brought about by allowing spiritual disciplines to modify our habits. The best way to break a habit is to drop it. But that takes considerable effort. Effort which, by the way, is not in any kind of conflict with God's grace. This is, after all, God at work in us. Grace on God's part is not denied by effort on our part. It's only if we should think that our effort is earning us anything, that the conflict arises.

Christian living is a matter of life or death. That's the Apostle Paul's biblical teaching. It stems from becoming meditatively aware (mindful) of the invisible reality of our being in union with Christ. In the context of a body dead in Adam; we have a spirit alive in Christ. In this we find the classic paradox of an authentic Christian experience. It's about a kind of life that leads to death; but it's also about a kind of death that leads to life. No, I'm not talking about false human distortions of Bible teaching:

neither masochism nor asceticism. Instead, it's about taking up our cross and crucifying our fallen nature (Gal.5:24) – which we do by the Spirit's agency (see Romans 8:13). We discipline ourselves to turn from evil by no longer making provision for the lusts of the flesh (Romans 13:14).

Although we rightly would refer back to our Lord's instructive Sermon of the Mount when he spoke figuratively about gouging out our eye and cutting off our hand as the means of regulating our viewing and tempering our actions, we should make it clear we're not talking about us modifying our own behaviour without first altering our thinking (Proverbs 23:7). The Bible makes that need obvious when it introduces the topic of character transformation by an initial focus on the need to take our mind off worldly things and deliberately become more constantly aware of heavenly realities (Romans 8:5; Colossians 3:1). Only then does it command us to put off certain vices and to equally put on replacement virtues. These virtues are nothing short of the mind of Christ (1 Corinthians 2:16; Philippians 2); the affections of Christ (Philippians 1:8); and the love of Christ (2 Corinthians 5:14).

As an aside, may I ask you to visualize one of the tricks used by political satirists. Like me, you've probably seen photographs of, let's say, a U.S. President; photographs which have been modified, or photoshopped, as we say today. It may have started out originally as a photograph of Bill Clinton, but now when you look at it you can convince yourself you might as well be looking at a photograph of President Bush. One photograph has been morphed into the other, and at the halfway stage between the two, there are as many recognizable features of the one leader as there are of the other.

I'm reminded of those words spoken by John the Baptist on the banks of the Jordan river. Referring to Jesus Christ, he said: "he must increase and I must decrease". That's the way to bring about increasing likeness to Christ in our lives too. But there's no computer program that can help us do that. Rather it has to be a Bible-based program of mortification. That's not something that gets much talked about these days. And if it does, it may well be misunderstood. When the Bible speaks about this – and it does – it most certainly isn't describing any kind of religiously motivated self-harm! We're to glorify God in these bodies of ours, not to harm them in any way (1 Corinthians 6:19,20).

What then is mortification? Both Romans chapter 8 and Colossians chapter 3 mention this. Sometimes, it's translated in such a way as it tells us to consider our members which are on the earth as being dead to such things as immorality, impurity, passion, evil desire and greed - and so rid them from our experience. This doesn't happen overnight, nor is it automatic as a result of making a one-time commitment to Christ. But it's a daily, repeated - habitual - putting off of self. Realistically, this is only achievable if we are continually mindful of our union with Christ. And that happens, as we've said, by intentionally bringing to mind, and concentrating on, exalted things: things that are consistent with the risen life of our Lord above, who is seated at God's right hand. And mortification, the putting off of unworthy behaviours, needs to be accompanied by the spiritual process of renewal which is the putting on of Christ. As we mentioned before, these replacement virtues are nothing short of the mind of Christ (1 Corinthians 2:16; Philippians 2); the affections of Christ (Philippians 1:8); and the love of Christ (2 Corinthians 5:14).

On that point emphasizing 'love,' we scan down the fifth chapter of Paul's letter to the Galatians in order to remind ourselves how love heads up the listing of the fruit of the Spirit. God is love (1 John 4:8); love is the summation of the law (Romans 13:10); and love frames the lists of Christian virtues we find in places like 2 Peter 1; Colossians 3; as well as in Galatians 5:

> "But I say, walk by the Spirit, and you will not carry out the desire of the flesh. For the flesh sets its desire against the Spir-

it, and the Spirit against the flesh; for these are in opposition to one another, so that you may not do the things that you please. But if you are led by the Spirit, you are not under the Law. Now the deeds of the flesh are evident, which are: immorality, impurity, sensuality, idolatry, sorcery, enmities, strife, jealousy, outbursts of anger, disputes, dissensions, factions, envying, drunkenness, carousing, and things like these, of which I forewarn you, just as I have forewarned you, that those who practice such things will not inherit the kingdom of God.

But the fruit of the Spirit is love, joy, peace, patience, kindness, goodness, faithfulness, gentleness, self-control; against such things there is no law. Now those who belong to Christ Jesus have crucified the flesh with its passions and desires. If we live by the Spirit, let us also walk by the Spirit. Let us not become boastful, challenging one another, envying one another" (Galatians 5:16-26).

Spiritual transformation is the combined process of mortification and renewal by which the elements of our character take on the elements of Christ's character – his mind (1 Corinthians 2:16), will (1 Peter 4:2), and emotions (Philippians 1:8).

I'm not sure if we take this seriously enough. What if we were to ask each other: 'What is your mortification program?' Makeover programs make for fashionable TV viewing. Our curiosity is stimulated to see the difference in the appearance of a person or a car or a house or garden after a team of consultants and experts get to work on changing its appearance. When did we last show as much interest in a makeover of our character?

CHAPTER SIX: REVIEW QUESTIONS

1. Why is renewal of our mind key?
2. Which Bible passages would you use to defend the statement that 'mindfulness of our union with Christ is a life-transforming truth'?
3. How seriously have you taken the biblical discipline of 'mortification'? How would you put into words your understanding of what Col.3:5 & Rom.8:13 are asking you to do?
4. Our destiny is to share a family likeness to God's son. With that as motivation, let's ask each other: 'What is your "mortification program"?'

LIKE A RIVER GLORIOUS

Like a river glorious is God's perfect peace,

Over all victorious, in its bright increase;

Perfect, yet it floweth fuller every day,

Perfect, yet it groweth deeper all the way.

Hidden in the hollow of His blessed hand,

Never foe can follow, never traitor stand;

Not a surge of worry, not a shade of care,

Not a blast of hurry, touch the spirit there.

Every joy or trial falleth from above,

Traced upon life's dial by the Sun of Love;

We may trust Him fully, all for us to do;

They who trust Him wholly find Him wholly true.

Stayed upon Jehovah, hearts are fully blest

Finding, as He promised, perfect peace and rest.

(F.R. Havergal)

CHAPTER SEVEN: USING THE 'SIMPLEST' METHOD OF TRANSFORMATION

Slowing down from the frenetic pace of modern living; reducing stress by becoming aware of our body's stress signs; enjoying the moment whether it be a sunset or birdsong; having a heightened awareness of our thoughts and feelings - for example, when catching ourselves unhelpfully brooding on something; tuning into and enjoying more of what's going on around us ... these would all generally be considered as being good things in themselves. What's more, they're even endorsed by the British National Health Service these days under the banner heading of 'mindfulness.' While some might reject all value in such things because they smack too much of self-absorption, or maybe even because of the suspected Buddhist origins of this modern trend, others ask: 'what if a Christian version of it should capture the idea of basking in our beliefs, holding scriptures in our mind, and connecting more deeply with God in our lives as we journey through each day one moment at a time?'

Actually, the Bible has long encouraged us to be mindful of the things of God. It instructs us where our thoughts should be concentrated. Distraction is a problem in Christian living. The things of the here and now tend to press themselves upon us, taking our focus away from eternal realities. Many times, we find ourselves having to renew our perspective. The Apostle Paul talked about the things that are seen being temporal; while the eternal things are unseen (2 Corinthians 4). When I hear those words of Paul, I always think about a time when my wife and I were living in Belgium as part of a church-planting mission there. A group of friends came over from the UK to support a baptismal event we were hosting. The party included the elderly parents of a colleague, a fine Christian couple. The next morning, the visiting group leader had planned an early start to take in some sightseeing. The elderly Christian gentleman turned to me with a resigned smile, saying: 'That which is seen is temporal ...' I doubt he was set against relaxing for a short while amid pleasant scenery, but he was very clearly mindful that there were more valuable experiences. If it seemed a little surreal at the time, it's rebuked me since, as this is the true perspective on Christian living.

It did serve as a reminder of something I'd personally experienced as a young man. During the years I spent at university – years which I thoroughly enjoyed – I have the fondest memories of times I spent in the evenings, seeking communion with God. After all the tutorial work was completed, I'd jump in my car and drive a few miles into the countryside to a picturesque scene involving a body of water set over against the sinking evening sun. I think it may have been known as Gladhouse reservoir, but that matters little. The point was that it was a peaceful backdrop which displayed something of the handiwork of God. I'd then set a Scripture in Song cassette tape into the rather tinny-sounding car-player and prepared to read my Bible. It wasn't that I was previously unfamiliar with Bible-reading, but this was a new experience: I felt I was drawing close to God, or rather that he was drawing close to me. These times became very precious. They cultivated in me a sense of God that was far in excess of anything I'd previously known. The Bible came alive to me.

The Bible is the living and active Word of God, so I guess what I'm really saying is that I became more alive to it. I was absorbed in the reading of it. If I'd some measure of grip of it before; it now had a grip of me – and there's a big difference between those two things! I scarcely realized it then, but I look back now on those times as being formative times in my life – more valuable than the academic training taking place by day. I was beginning to experience what it means to delight in God and to have your heart's desires shaped by him. It sparked my enthusiasm for the endeavour, at least, of leading others to Christ and planting biblical churches of God. Little by little, other career goals receded.

What I'm saying is that this was my first taste of becoming mindful of the things that really matter – a small personal step in seeing revival turn into reformation by means of the renewing of my mind through having its perceptions adjusted gradually by values absorbed from God's Word. As I look back on it now, I'd like to share in some more detail what I'm calling the S.I.M.P.L.E.S.T way to become what we are in Christ. It's how I now regard the process with the help of the Bible's teaching on it. The name 'SIMPLEST' is an acronym, where each letter stands for a relevant word in the description of the method. 'S' stands for 'Spirit,' and the point to associate with this is that we must begin our quest by prayerfully orientating our human spirit to God's Spirit – for that's the way for us to receive God's revelation (Romans 8:16; 1 Corinthians 2:12; Psalm 19:7).

The 'I' and the 'M' stand for 'Intent of Mind'. This describes reading the Scriptures intently – with the aim of rebooting our mind with the knowledge of truth (1 Timothy 2:4). It's in this way that we come to learn Christ (Ephesians 4:20), leaving behind previous futile forms of thinking when we were mainly mindful of other things, and not the things of God.

So, 'S' for Spirit, our own human spirit, and 'I' and 'M' for Intent of Mind. Those are the first three letters of SIMPLEST. And next, the 'P' stands for 'Penetrates' the heart – which is what God's truth does when our mind is set on God's things. As we meditate on the Bible's teaching, committing to memory the truth set before our mind, so its values filter down into the core of our being where it will begin to influence our lifestyle choices. This is where we pick up the 'L' and 'E' of SIMPLEST, drawing them as first and last from the word 'LifE'. The heart, at the centre of our lives, is where we reflect on God's things with 'purpose of heart' until they come to shape our will (Proverbs 23:7), and we submit our 'mortified' body (Romans 12:1) as poised to do good, for productive outcomes in our life. Our Soul's Transformation is now underway. By the way, that's the 'S T' that completes our acronym: SIMPLEST – it's the 'S' and the 'T' from the initials of Soul's Transformation. We are now ready to display modified behaviour in the life of our soul – this being the result of processing our altered thinking (Romans 8; Colossians 3; 2 Peter 1; Galatians 5).

Remember, we said it all starts with the mind, with being mindful of the things of God. If we take it this way, the current trending of the word 'mindfulness' serves as a helpful warning of how we must try to avoid getting the same rebuke the Apostle Peter received from the Lord. The Lord, you'll recall, told him frankly that he was not mindful of the things of God.

The step by step procedure can once more be summarized as: prayerfully orienting our human **Spirit** to the Spirit of God - preparing prayerfully to receive God's revelation, his communication through his Word. Then, read the Scriptures – it begins with an intellectual exercise as we first attempt to understand what we read (Acts 8:30,31) in order to engage the mind with the knowledge of truth (1 Timothy 2:4). And this is helped if we commit a daily text to memory. So, we set the **Mind** - setting ultimate truth before it; grasping its significance. This brings into play the **Heart** which is where we allow truth to penetrate down into; this being the seat of meditative reflection; and, if you will, it's the 'central processor' that shapes our will. All this then issues forth in the Life of our **Soul** – helping us to live in the truth; not only knowing it, but applying it to transform our behaviour.

We are complete in Christ, but isn't this how the Bible itself instructs us how we become in daily life what we already are by the grace of God in his sight? It instructs us to be mindful at all times of our Christian identity and character (Romans 8; Colossians 3; Galatians 5; 2 Peter 1). Of course, we can't do this ourselves, it's only by working with God. We obviously need God's help, for no-one can crucify himself or herself.

Mortification is a forgotten Christian discipline. It's all about recognising evil and refusing it, by setting the mind on higher things in order to bring our body into submission such that it becomes poised to do good - not by force of will – but by spiritual disciplines. These disciplines are about breaking bad habits and making good habits. It helps us to turn from evil when we make no provision for the lusts of the flesh (Romans 13:14). Negatively, it's by figuratively gouging out our eye, and cutting off our hand or foot (Matthew 5:29,30); more positively, it's by setting our mind on things above, things of the Spirit of God (Romans 8:5; Colossians 3:1; Philippians 4:8) – so it's both by putting off what's inconsistent and putting on what's consistent with the life of our risen Lord.

Daily, God's Word in the power of his Spirit enters the mind and filters down into our heart and there shapes our will to produce change in the life of our soul. Spiritual transformation is this overall process by which all the elements of self take on the character of the elements of Christ.

CHAPTER SEVEN: REVIEW QUESTIONS

1. What is it in our lifestyle that hinders us from connecting more deeply with God at any moment?
2. That which is immediate and all around us, inviting our attention, naturally becomes our focus. How is it possible to retain Paul's perspective of the eternal (and invisible) over against the temporal that is nonetheless highly visible?
3. Is there a time we can recall when we seemed to break through to a deeper sense of God? What factors facilitated this?
4. Think through the various steps of the SIMPLEST method - what stage presents the highest level of challenge for you?

O BLESSED GOD HOW KIND

O Blessed God, how kind

Are all they ways to me,

Whose dark benighted mind

Was enmity to Thee!

Yet now, subdued by sovereign grace,

My spirit longs for Your embrace.

How precious are Your thoughts,

That o'er my spirit roll,

They swell beyond my faults

And captivate my soul!

How great their sum, how high they rise,

Can ne'er be known beneath the skies.

(Anon.)

CHAPTER EIGHT: ACHIEVING SOBERNESS OF MIND

There's a particular word that's found 4 times in the New Testament; and it's a word that's directed towards what should be the expected behaviour of believers on the Lord Jesus (Strong's number 4993, literally meaning: 'safe or sound or sober in mind'). It would be good if we could look at the context of each of these occurrences so as to discover if we're mindful of displaying this quality or not. The first we'll look at is found in First Peter chapter 4, where Peter says:

> "Therefore, since Christ has suffered in the flesh, arm yourselves also with the same purpose, because he who has suffered in the flesh has ceased from sin, so as to live the rest of the time in the flesh no longer for the lusts of men, but for the will of God. For the time already past is sufficient for you to have carried out the desire of the Gentiles, having pursued a course of sensuality, lusts, drunkenness, carousing, drinking parties and abominable idolatries. In all this, they are surprised that you do not run with them into the same excesses of dissipation, and they malign you; but they will give account to Him who is ready to judge the living and the dead. For the gospel has for

this purpose been preached even to those who are dead, that though they are judged in the flesh as men, they may live in the spirit according to the will of God. The end of all things is near; therefore, be of sound judgment and sober spirit for the purpose of prayer" (1 Peter 4:1-7).

That last part should get our attention. Here's the state of mind we need to get ourselves into if we wish our prayers to be effective. There's a right time for laughter, of course, and we're called to rejoice in an appropriate way at all times, but light-heartedness doesn't commend us to God in prayer. Prayer is such a significant privilege that we need to take it seriously. We're on the earth and we're speaking with the sovereign majesty on high. Prayer is for people who are thinking soberly.

Now, a little bit of context. We appreciate this was first written by the Apostle Peter to believers with their backs to the wall under the Roman Emperor, Nero, and his insanely cruel torture of Christians. Appropriately, and very poignantly, Peter brings before his original readers the example of Jesus, the Suffering Servant. Some folks today think that suffering is a kind of indicator that something is lacking in a Christian's life – often a lack of faith is blamed for it if it should happen to intrude into the life of a Christian believer. But nothing could be further from the biblical truth. The message through Peter here is that certain kinds of suffering are inevitable in this world, and our appropriate response is to allow ourselves to be shaped by it. The God who allows suffering to come into our lives, does so because he desires it to have the effect of causing us to stop sinning as much, and to live more in the centre of God's will for us.

Suffering, as Peter remarkably presents it here, is seen as a positive opportunity for acquiring the mind of Christ. In other words, arming ourselves with the same attitude as Christ showed when he lived on earth, overcoming in all the things he suffered. In turn, this results in a God-honouring lifestyle, perhaps quite radically different from the lifestyle we were pursuing before our conversion. In stark relief to hedonism running wild; a Christian's right mind is seen to be a serious determination to do God's will – by going his way. A determination to please the Lord in life is the sort of determination that's often sharpened by the experience of suffering. And it may be part of the answer as to why God permits such things to enter our lives in the first place. The bigger picture, as it were, despite these experiences – unpleasant in themselves – being things we'd sooner avoid.

The next verse I want to draw your attention to, another which contains the same word, is in Titus, in chapter 2, verse 6, which simply says: "Likewise urge the young men to be sensible [or self-controlled]." Actually, this same word group appears no less than five times in Paul's letter to his colleague, Titus (see 1:8;2:2,5,12). Prior to conversion, Paul says in the surrounding verses (in Titus 3:3), that we were found serving our own lusts and pleasures. In fact, some in the churches of God in Crete, reflecting their own culture, were still letting some of the traits of their old lifestyle show through. These were things like insubjection, unruly behaviour, speaking evil of people, not being peaceable, gentle, humble, even deceiving as well as corrupting and being corrupted by greed. Although those Paul was describing here to Titus were believers, they most certainly weren't in their right mind (as the man with the legion of demons came to be in Luke 8:35)! What's meant by a right or sober mind is what's defined throughout the letter to Titus. It's very different to the prevailing general characteristics that had been described. A right mind is an awareness – a mindfulness – of the need to always be subject, submissive, moderate, controlled, loyal and true, dealing honestly – in other words, overall, having a submissive and self-controlled attitude.

We now come to the time Paul used the word in writing to the believers at Corinth. In his second letter to them, chapter 5, he said:

"We are not again commending ourselves to you but are giving you an occasion to be proud of us, so that you will have an answer for those who take pride in appearance and not in heart. For if we are beside ourselves, it is for God; if we are of sound mind, it is for you. For the love of Christ controls us, having concluded this, that one died for all, therefore all died; and He died for all, so that they who live might no longer live for themselves, but for Him who died and rose again on their behalf" (2 Corinthians 5:12-15).

In this verse, Paul acknowledges that some might take him for a madman - with a holy madness or religious mania expressed in his commitment - but it's equally clear that he regarded himself as sober-minded, for though they were so indebted to him, he still wasn't inclined to boast about this. Apart from this self-effacing attitude, what other characteristics of his sober mind shine through this section stretching back to the latter part of chapter four? Surely, it's the balancing perspective of present afflictions weighed over against eternal glory. It was Paul's ambition, as it should also be ours, to please the Lord in the light of his soon-to-happen return – a time when Christian believers will each get a new body to replace this present one with its daily decay of faculties. The message of Paul here, we might say, adds up to a mindfulness of spiritual perspectives and ambitions.

Finally, we come to Romans chapter 12:

"For through the grace given to me I say to everyone among you not to think more highly of himself than he ought to think; but to think so as to have sound judgment, as God has allotted to each a measure of faith. For just as we have many members in one body and all the members do not have the same function, so we, who are many, are one body in Christ, and individually members one of another. Since we have gifts that differ according to the grace given to us ... [let us use them]" (Romans 12:3-6).

Here we find a humble mind, with soberness revealed in thinking of ourselves no more highly than is proper! In other words, having a straight-thinking and honest appraisal of ourselves. When we put it all together from each of the four places where we find it discussed in the New Testament, here's the picture that we should be fully aware of: we're to live in a dignified way in a pain-filled world, ready to engage meaningfully in prayer; we're to be in control of ourselves at all times as the Spirit of God enables us; having long-term perspectives and ambitions that reach way beyond the here and now; and we're to be very honest and realistic in the estimate we hold about ourselves in relation to others whom we're to readily concede as having valuable contributions to make.

Now that is true Christian mindfulness! That's the kind of mindfulness that our Lord endorses in his Word.

CHAPTER EIGHT: REVIEW QUESTIONS

1. What is the danger of a carefree life?
2. How can we help prevent cultural characteristics from dominating us?
3. In what ways can a longer term (even eternal) perspective help us to achieve a self-effacing attitude in the here and now – especially when workplace pressures may demand the opposite?
4. At any time when we've been self-aware and managed to practise giving way to others through an honest appraisal of ourselves – only to be disappointed by the reaction of others – how did we feel and how did we overcome this feeling?

TAKE MY LIFE AND LET IT BE

Take my life and let it be

Consecrated, Lord, to Thee.

Take my moments and my days,

Let them flow in endless praise.

Take my hands and let them move

At the impulse of Thy love.

Take my feet and let them be

Swift and beautiful for Thee.

Take my will and make it Thine,

It shall be no longer mine.

Take my heart, it is Thine own,

It shall be Thy royal throne.

Take my love, my Lord, I pour

At Thy feet its treasure store.

Take myself and let me be

Ever, only, all for Thee.

(F.R. Havergal)

CHAPTER NINE: EXERCISING A LISTENING AND DISCERNING MIND

Do you remember what it was that king David's son Solomon asked for when God appeared to him and invited him to request of him whatever he wanted? This was at the beginning of his reign. We read:

> "In Gibeon the LORD appeared to Solomon in a dream at night; and God said, "Ask what you wish me to give you." Then Solomon said, "... O LORD my God, You have made Your servant king in place of my father David, yet I am but a little child; I do not know how to go out or come in. Your servant is in the midst of Your people which You have chosen, a great people who are too many to be numbered or counted. So give Your servant **an understanding heart** to judge Your people **to discern between good and evil**. For who is able to judge this great people of Yours?" (1 Kings 3:5-9).

Were you caught out by that answer? Perhaps you thought that Solomon asked for wisdom. Well, God gave him that as well. For since his request was pleasing to God, God replied: "I have given you a wise and discerning heart" (1 Kings 3:12b). In some Bible versions, the alternative marginal readings clarify that when Solomon asked for an understanding heart, it could more literally have been expressed as asking for a 'listening heart.' Of course, that begs the question: listening to what? Solomon wanted a heart that was tuned in to God's Law or God's Word. There's always wisdom in doing that. The Bible repeats this good advice: "Today ... hear his voice" (Psalm 95:7). We hear God's voice by paying close attention to what he says to us in the Bible. The opening verses of Isaiah chapter 66 tell us:

> "Thus says the LORD, "Heaven is My throne and the earth is My footstool. Where then is a house you could build for Me? And where is a place that I may rest? For My hand made all these things, thus all these things came into being," declares the LORD. "But to this one I will look, to him who is humble and contrite of spirit, and who trembles at My word" (Isaiah 66:1-2).

That is, if we want to grab God's attention, all we need to do is to humbly accept God's Word (Isaiah 66:1,2) and let it hold sway over all the world's views. In other words, to let God be true and every man a liar (Romans 3:4). Let's not undervalue the pleasure God gets when we read and respect his Word. I remember a story from Tucson, U.S. A man brings an old blanket to the US edition of the Antiques Roadshow – a popular television program where people are invited to bring items from their homes to be valued by experts. People are always hoping they'll discover they're holding onto something far more valuable than they'd ever imagined. Well, as we said, this particular chap brought an old blanket - something he had regarded as commonplace. When the expert saw it, however, his eyes lit up! For this was a blanket that had once belonged to a Navajo Indian Chief around 1840. Suddenly, this item was transformed in its owner's eyes. Perhaps he'd arrived with it slung over his arm, but now with a $500,000 valuation placed on it, he left in the company of security guards! Something regarded as commonplace had been suddenly transformed.

Sometimes, perhaps, our Bible-reading discipline can seem a little forced, there may be times when we hardly seem to be enjoying it – even begin to wonder if it's worth it. May our valuation of what pleases God be radically revised upward – like the man with his antique blanket! Remember, it's those who rediscover the immense value of God's Word who get God's attention.

Summing up so far, what we've seen with Solomon is that an 'understanding heart' was in effect a listening mind. A mind constantly listening to God. Too often, we listen to the world around us. We absorb uncritically the views of our peers. And we all too readily let them dictate to us what's fair and normal. Genesis (1:1) tells us all we need to understand about origins; and Leviticus (18:22) informs us what we need to know about same-sex marriage. Listening to God's Word makes us to be able to discern what pleases him. At the close of Hebrews chapter 5, the writer informs us that: "... solid food is for the mature, for those who have their powers of discernment trained by constant practice to distinguish good from evil" (Hebrews 5:14 ESV). Notice what this verse does. It discloses that discernment is the evidence of maturity. And that discernment gets trained as we practise critically thinking through what to like and what not to like. When we distinguish carefully between what's true and what's false; and what's good and what's evil.

Shockingly, today some Christians consider spiritual immaturity to be the mark of authenticity – 'don't trouble me with doctrine or theology, they say, just give me Jesus.' Actually, if we were to ask them: 'Who is Jesus?' they would inevitably have to give us a theological or doctrinal answer! But immaturity isn't the way to go. We're not to remain shallow in our understanding of God's Word, even although mere head knowledge isn't what we're aiming for.

Maturity is inseparable from discernment, and the immediate context in Hebrews 5 shows us that we need to become skilled in the Word – which brings us back to the great value of it that we were thinking about earlier. The Hebrew Christians being addressed here weren't skilled or trained in God's Word, and they had to be told that they were going back or regressing in the Christian life – or, at very least, they weren't able to take the next steps. This was far from progress. God wants us to advance beyond the basics – and that demands us becoming trained in distinguishing between good and evil. The benefit this brings is that mature discernment is a defence against counterfeit learning and compromised living.

We're to discern what pleases God, what fulfils his will, and what is consistent with Scripture. This level of discernment is developed by practice, as we distinguish between what's better and what's best (according to Philippians 1:10); between what's good and evil (according to Romans 16:19); and between what's holy and profane (Leviticus 10:10). Maturity in Christian life is about learning how to distinguish between true and false, between good and bad, between right and wrong. The reason this isn't easy, and takes maturity, is because the Devil is a master counterfeiter. He specializes in masking the difference between what's genuine and what's counterfeit. Copying what God does, is what the Devil specializes in. No counterfeiter would make a $99 bill, but only an expertly crafted forgery of a $100 bill! It's not meant to be easy to detect.

A new £5 note has been recently introduced in the UK. Checking for counterfeit notes involves a total of 10 checks by touching, tilting, and both looking at and through it. But forgery isn't a new problem, of course. Back in the Greek world there were rogue money-traders. Only some money-traders were approved or 'dokimos' – a word found with this meaning in the New Testament. Money then was worth its face-value in actual weight (from which we get the expression that something is 'worth its weight in gold'). A favourite trick then was to shave off very slight amounts of gold from many coins until you had enough to make a new additional one. Repeat this procedure often enough and you could literally 'make money.' So, to take up the way the Bible applies this word 'approved,' we find Romans 14:22 saying: "Happy is he who does not condemn himself in what he approves."

Coming back to our overall theme of mindfulness, we should be mindful at all times of our Christian identity. A practical way we can apply this can be found in the area of social media. It can be so easy to condemn ourselves by our Facebook 'likes.' This happens when we approve something without thinking through if it conforms to biblical standards, as opposed to expressing the world's view. We can become so accustomed to the latter, that we fail to pause and check if what we're liking is really appropriate for someone representing Christianity. In that way, it comes back to being at all times mindful of our Christian identity.

CHAPTER NINE: REVIEW QUESTIONS

1. Share some significant benefits of a disciplined Bible-reading program.
2. Why, do you think, maturity is shown to be marked by a quality of discernment?
3. How can we help ourselves to take more seriously the need to approve the same things that God approves?
4. What, do you think, Phil.1:10 is saying (hint: note the NIV rendering)?

BE STILL MY SOUL

Be still, my soul; the Lord is on thy side;

Bear patiently the cross of grief or pain;

Leave to thy God to order and provide;

In every change He faithful will remain.

Be still, my soul; thy best, thy heavenly, Friend

Through thorny ways leads to a joyful end.

Be still, my soul; thy God doth undertake

To guide the future as He has the past.

Thy hope, thy confidence, let nothing shake;

All now mysterious shall be bright at last.

Be still, my soul; the waves and winds still know

His voice who ruled them while He dwelt below.

(Catharina von Schlegel)

CHAPTER TEN: HAVING THE MIND AND ATTITUDE OF CHRIST

There were a number of reasons for Paul writing his letter to the Church of God at Philippi. It evidently was concerning to Paul that there was a failure on the part of some believers there to pull together as harmoniously as could be desired (Philippians 1:14-17, 27; 2:2ff.; 4:2,3). He urges them to reach agreement with one another and to pull together in joyful teamwork. Paul's diagnosis was that if each put the interests of others before his or her own interests - if there was a greater willingness to make concessions – then all would be well. He begins chapter 2 by saying:

> "Therefore if there is any encouragement in Christ, if there is any consolation of love, if there is any fellowship of the Spirit, if any affection and compassion, make my joy complete by being of the same mind, maintaining the same love, united in spirit, intent on one purpose. Do nothing from selfishness or empty conceit, but with humility of mind regard one another as more important than yourselves; do not merely look out for your own personal interests, but also for the interests of others" (Philippians 2:1-4).

And it was to reinforce this that Paul quoted some now famous Bible lines which celebrate the humiliation to which Christ voluntarily submitted himself in becoming man and dying on the cross. I say he 'quotes' them, for it's been widely agreed that in Philippians 2:6-11 we find an early Christian hymn fragment or poetic composition - whether Paul's own work or someone else's. Paul quotes it here to give his call to unity the greatest possible support. He continues by saying:

> "Have this attitude in yourselves which was also in Christ Jesus, who, although He existed in the form of God, did not regard equality with God a thing to be grasped, but emptied Himself, taking the form of a bond-servant, and being made in the likeness of men. Being found in appearance as a man, He humbled Himself by becoming obedient to the point of death, even death on a cross. For this reason also, God highly exalted Him, and bestowed on Him the name which is above every name, so that at the name of Jesus EVERY KNEE WILL BOW, of those who are in heaven and on earth and under the earth, and that every tongue will confess that Jesus Christ is Lord, to the glory of God the Father" (Philippians 2:5-11).

In itself this passage is a recital of the saving work of God in Christ - in his incarnation, passion and exaltation. But there's a major difference here. What is it, you ask? It's the context in which this is quoted. That's what brings fresh significance to the actions of Christ as they're rehearsed here. Remember, Paul's target here is some measure of disharmony among the Christian believers at Philippi. He'd already confronted disunity at Corinth, and dealt with it in the very first chapter of his first biblical letter to them. When doing that, he'd also taken them directly to the cross. Again, here, Paul's Spirit-directed instinct is to go to the cross to ground his appeal in the most heartfelt terms. But there's a difference here. Paul introduces this poetic summary by saying: "Have this attitude in yourselves which was also in Christ Jesus ..." (Philippians 2:5).

In other words, the attitude shown by Christ is recommended as an example for his followers. Jesus' attitude is presented as an example of what the Philippians' attitude should be, and they're being encouraged 'to become like him in his death' (Philippians 3:10). This is what Paul meant earlier when asking them to 'decide what is best' (Philippians 1:10). This is the best mindset to adopt. So here, in Philippians chapter 2, it's not so much the actions of Christ but the attitude behind them which is the focus. And by God's help we – as well as they – are to try to copy it. Attitude has always been as important, if not more important, to God than any actions a person may do.

God recorded in the Bible books of Chronicles those kings which did the right things; and those kings who not only did the right things but did them with the right attitude or with their 'whole heart' (e.g. Amaziah in 2 Chronicles 25:2). So, it's right for us to praise God as much for the wonderful attitude of Christ as it is to praise God for the wonderful actions of Christ.

In Philippians chapter 2, one commentator (J. B. Lightfoot) paraphrases the opening in this way: 'He, though existing before the worlds in the form of God, did not treat His equality with God as a prize, [as] a treasure to be greedily clutched and ostentatiously displayed: on the contrary, He resigned the glories of heaven'- and he adds that 'this is the common and indeed almost universal interpretation of the Greek fathers, who would have the most lively sense of the requirements of the language.'

Despite having equality with the Father as his eternal right, the Son of God - revealed to us as Jesus – didn't regard equality with God as a vantage-point for achieving his personal ambitions. Precisely the opposite, in fact! He actually treated his equality with God as an occasion for renouncing every advantage or privilege to which he was entitled. We can easily think of people we know, either personally or from the pages of history, who've used whatever position of authority they'd been given to selfishly satisfy their own lust for more power, more fame, more wealth etc. – using their privileged status for their own advantage. How different it was with Jesus! He regarded his equality with God as an opportunity not for self-enrichment but for self-impoverishment and unreserved self-sacrifice. This is so amazing that it has confused some into rejecting his equality with God. How tragic! For this should be the very pinnacle of our praise!

This isn't the only place where Paul points to Christ's self-denial as being an example for his people. 2 Corinthians 8:9 is another place, for example, where Paul encourages generous giving to the Jerusalem relief fund by supplying as an incentive "the grace of our Lord Jesus Christ who, though he was rich, yet for your sakes became poor, that through his poverty you might become rich". There, he uses his own language, but here, in Philippians 2:6-11, he appears to have used a readily available form of words.

As we think again of how the Lord Jesus Christ regarded his equality with God as an opportunity, not for self-enrichment, but for self-impoverishment and unreserved self-sacrifice, we learn something of the very essence of the humble mind of Christ. Of course, this extended way back before he became also a man. This in the eternal attitude of the second person of the Trinity, and as such, true of the divine being. If only we could live in the constant awareness of this, and let it moderate our own actions moment by moment, that would indeed be true Christian mindfulness!

I'm sure the eleven disciples were always mindful of what they had so tellingly observed in the upper room when the Lord had got up from supper and washed their feet. An unforgettable action! They must have spent their lives reflecting on the immense humility that lay behind it, for some at least had equally witnessed his excellent majesty shining as the sun in its strength. In Kendrick's memorable words: 'This is our God, the Servant King.' In the upper room, the Lord had said that what he'd done was to be an example for them. Let's be totally aware, the implication for us too, is: 'Go, and do likewise'!

Chuck Swindoll writes: 'Attitude, to me, is more important than education, than money, than circumstances, than failures, than successes, than what other people think or say or do. It's more important than appearance, giftedness, or skill ... we have a choice every day regarding the attitude we embrace for that day ... I'm convinced that life is 10 per cent what happens to me and 90 per cent how I react to it. And so it is with you ... We are in charge of our attitudes.' Paul writes, "You must have the same attitude that Christ Jesus had.' He always approached people with love, grace, acceptance, and a heart to serve rather than be served.

CHAPTER TEN: REVIEW QUESTIONS

1. What's the distinguishing mark of the sharing of the cross-work of Christ that we find in Philippians chapter 2?
2. If actions speak louder than words, would it be correct to add – but attitude speaks even louder? Why?
3. We are tempted to think of 'any job having its perks' (that is, advantages that we feel entitled to enjoy as a result of reaching a hard-earned position). Is this a valid Christian mindset? Why, or why not?
4. In practice, how may we choose or select an attitude?

LORD JESUS, YOU WHO ONLY

Lord Jesus, You who only are

The endless source of purest joy,

O come and fill this longing heart;

May none but You my thoughts employ.

Teach me on You to fix my eye,

For none but You can satisfy.

The joys of earth can never fill

The heart that's tasted of Your love;

No portion would I seek until

I reign with You, my Lord, above,

When I shall gaze upon Your face,

And know more fully all Your grace.

Till You shall come to take me home,

Be this my one ambition, Lord,

Self, sin, the world, to overcome,

Fast clinging to Your faithful Word;

More of Yourself each day to know,

And more into Your image grow.

CHAPTER ELEVEN: BEING MINDFUL OF WHAT ULTIMATELY MATTERS

We earlier remembered Jesus' rebuke to Simon Peter when Peter had tried to dissuade Jesus from talking in terms of dying at Jerusalem. The Lord had said then that Peter was not being mindful of God's things. We now want to turn that around, and by reading the Gospels as they report the words of our Lord, we try to discover what it means in practice to be mindful of the things that matter to God.

Of course, that exchange with Peter immediately showed that the Lord was always mindful of his death. Early in his ministry here on earth, he spoke of it as a form of baptism that awaited him; and one that ever weighed upon his mind. The Apostle John saw into heaven as he recounts in chapter 5, verse 1 of the book of Revelation, and there he saw a vision of God appearing to hold a scroll in his hand; a scroll surely containing the judgements and plans God had for this world, as would unfold later throughout the detailed visions of the Book of Revelation. But to John it was graphically shown that there was no-one worthy enough to carry them out, no-one at all, even in heaven. This troubled John, until he was told to view someone described as a lion. However, when John turned to look, he in fact saw a lamb. Without doubt, this has got to be the greatest mixed metaphor that could ever be!

The Lord Jesus Christ is both - both the majestic and mighty lion and the sacrificial lamb. And because he is both, he is the only one worthy to fulfil all of God's plans for this world and the world to come. The cross of Christ is pivotal in God's eternal purpose. It underwrites everything. It was the Apostle Paul's boast (Galatians 6:14), and it will be for ever our theme, as is indicated in the Book of Revelation.

We sometimes sing the hymn that says, 'Jesus, keep me near the cross ...' We've already considered how the Bible explains that we died with Christ. This is the definition of a Christian: someone who has died and been raised in union with Christ, as a spiritual reality. To be as mindful of the cross, therefore, as our Lord was on earth, is what powers the kind of transformed life that God desires to see us living. This awareness of our union with Christ is the most far-reaching kind of mindfulness there can possibly be – and the one that has the richest benefit.

What else did Jesus model for us in his life here, in terms of his mindfulness of issues God is interested in? Very much linked to what we've already considered, is the theme of rescuing the lost – whether the lost are pictured as sick patients or scattered chicks or straying sheep or prodigal children or – and this is the one I want to develop – as potential worshippers whom the Father in heaven is seeking for. The greatest exponent of mindfulness in its purest sense was our Lord, as viewed in his life here on earth – which we look into by the help of the four Gospel writers whose work was, of course, superintended by God himself. As we trace the Lord's life to his death on the cross, we find there was a particular awareness that consumed him, a burning passionate awareness. We're first allowed to glimpse it when it surfaces during a visit by Jesus with his parents to the Jerusalem temple. Luke takes up the story towards the close of his second chapter:

"The Child continued to grow and become strong, increasing in wisdom; and the grace of God was upon Him. Now His parents went to Jerusalem every year at the Feast of the Passover. And when He became twelve, they went up there according to the custom of the Feast; and as they were returning, after spending the full number of days, the boy Jesus stayed behind in Jerusalem. But His parents were unaware of it, but supposed Him to be in the caravan, and went a day's journey; and they began looking for Him among their relatives and acquaintances. When they did not find Him, they returned to Jerusalem looking for Him.

Then, after three days they found Him in the temple, sitting in the midst of the teachers, both listening to them and asking them questions. And all who heard Him were amazed at His understanding and His answers. When they saw Him, they were astonished; and His mother said to Him, "Son, why have You treated us this way? Behold, Your father and I have been anxiously looking for You." And He said to them, "Why is it that you were looking for Me? Did you not know that I had to be in My Father's house?" (Luke 2:40-49).

Here is the first recorded expression of his human perception of his mission. At the age of twelve, he was mindfully aware of his purpose and destiny – and his Father's business concerned his house on earth which was, of course, the very setting for Jesus' words to his relieved parents that day. Later, the same awareness is made evident in the repetition of the same or similar words in the identical context. Jesus is again drawn to the Jerusalem temple, surely emulating perfectly the revelation enjoyed by the psalmist when he said that God loves the gates of Zion (Psalm 87:2). In God's design, what had taken shape at Jerusalem, originally at God's explicit direction, was a reflection of a reality in heaven itself. Let's turn now to what John writes in his second chapter:

"The Passover of the Jews was near, and Jesus went up to Jerusalem. And He found in the temple those who were selling oxen and sheep and doves, and the money changers seated at their tables. And He made a scourge of cords, and drove them all out of the temple, with the sheep and the oxen; and He poured out the coins of the money changers and overturned their tables; and to those who were selling the doves He said, "Take these things away; stop making My Father's house a place of business." His disciples remembered that it was written, "ZEAL FOR YOUR HOUSE WILL CONSUME ME." (John 2:13-17).

These traders were defacing the integrity of the reflection of the heavenly here on earth at that time. The preciousness of the place to his God and Father was something, of course, our Lord was always aware of, as someone mindful at all times of those things which ultimately matter to God. One of those things, perhaps almost supreme among them, as the Bible witnesses to it from cover to cover, is God's intense longing to live on earth in a special way among people who serve him with obedient hearts. In pursuit of that staggering desire, God himself had stepped down into humanity and was headed for the cross, and the hour of which John repeatedly writes. Take, for example, his record of the conversation Jesus had one day with a non-Jewish woman whose thirst was deeper than she at first realized. John tells us that ...

"The woman said to Him, "Sir, I perceive that You are a prophet. "Our fathers worshiped in this mountain, and you people say that in Jerusalem is the place where men ought to worship." Jesus *said to her, "Woman, believe Me, an hour is coming when neither in this mountain nor in Jerusalem will you worship the Father. "You worship what you do not know; we worship what we know, for salvation is from the Jews. "But an hour is coming, and now is, when the true worshipers will

worship the Father in spirit and truth; for such people the
Father seeks to be His worshipers. "God is spirit, and those
who worship Him must worship in spirit and truth" (John
4:19-24).

When the hour of his death, of which Jesus had spoken to that woman
drew close, Jesus talked again acknowledging the rejection he was facing
from the Jerusalem leaders, whom he described as builders: "Jesus said to
them, "Did you never read in the Scriptures, 'THE STONE WHICH
THE BUILDERS REJECTED, THIS BECAME THE CHIEF COR-
NER stone; THIS CAME ABOUT FROM THE LORD, AND IT IS
MARVELOUS IN OUR EYES'?" (Matthew 21:42).

Jesus was the stone. In resurrection, he was raised and exalted by God,
and laid in the ultimate, heavenly Zion above as the precious cornerstone
(1 Peter 2:1-9), the elevated cornerstone of a spiritual structure rising
from earth that would come to transcend all geographical boundaries.
This would turn out to be the spiritual movement detailed from the time
of the Acts of the Apostles forward – and one that found its expression in
Christ's followers who remained loyal to his teaching passed on through
his apostles, and left on record to this day in their New Testament writings. This is so that we can be part of the same thing, through the self-
same quality of obedience as the first Christians. The writer to the Hebrews put it like this in chapter 3, verse 6: "Christ [is] faithful as a Son
over His house - whose house we are, if we hold fast our confidence and
the boast of our hope firm until the end."

The same mindfulness with which Christ headed for the cross – that is,
mindfulness of the building of a house for God (one made up of worshipers) - is reflected here in the confidence and hope of which Christians today are to be passionately aware. Those who are especially mindful of that biblical condition consequently form God's spiritual house on

earth today. They are then mindful of that which Jesus himself was always mindful of.

CHAPTER ELEVEN: REVIEW QUESTIONS

1. Various hymns encourage the idea of returning regularly in thought to the scene of the cross. Why is this kind of mindfulness important?
2. From an early age as a boy, Jesus was evidently mindful of God's interests. Which divine interest, do you think, surfaces most in his earthly life?
3. What is the place of worship that the Lord envisaged in John 4? Who are associated (biblically) with it? How large does this feature in our agenda?
4. What, if any, is the connection between the confidence and hope of those worshipping biblically today and the interest of the Father in seeking worshippers? Jesus was clearly very mindful of the latter, are we?

SWEET THE MOMENTS, RICH IN BLESSING

Sweet the moments, rich in blessing,

Which before the cross we spend,

Life and health and peace possessing

From the sinner's dying Friend.

Here we rest in wonder, viewing

All our sins on Jesus laid;

And a full redemption flowing

From the sacrifice He made.

Oh, that near the cross abiding

We may to the Saviour cleave,

Nought from Him our hearts dividing,

All for him content to leave.

May we still, the cross discerning,

There for peace and comfort go,

There new wonders daily learning,

All the depths of mercy know.

(W. Shirley)

CHAPTER TWELVE: FOCUSING ON THE BEAUTY OF GOD'S GLORY

Before we lost the sense of morality being absolute, and more recently lost the sense that truth is absolute, we'd already long since lost the sense of beauty being absolute. After all, we've long contented ourselves with the idea that beauty is in the eye of the beholder. But is this what the Bible teaches? The Westminster confession says that our chief end is "to glorify God and enjoy him for ever". Would it be modifying that very much, I wonder, to suggest that our noblest ambition is to see the beauty of the Lord, and then to reflect it accurately in our lives? Is God's glory not simply the radiance of his substance? After all, he designed all atoms so that when they get excited they give off a chemical fingerprint which identifies them. With that in mind, might we not think of God's glory as the communication of his unmistakable beauty.

The divine Spirit's work is introduced in the Bible's opening verses, performing the ultimate makeover of the formlessness of the earth - which is how it initially appeared when the raw materials were first brought into existence. When God proceeded to work with them, the earth was perfectly beautiful at the completion of his 6-day creation work. The same divine Spirit later gave to Bezalel and Oholiab (Exodus 36:2) - within the portable temple project - the skill to give effect to God's creative designs as described in the Bible – creative designs which declared something of God's glory. In the future, he will far extend the range of artistry so that in the supreme beauty of the new earth everything will say glory - the whole earth will be filled with God's glory because all of it will then be God's temple (which is why it will need no specific temple within it). God's beautiful garden will be worldwide in extent; and the glory once constrained in a portable temple structure will be universal. God will be all in all, and everything will be eternally beautiful.

Our concluding thoughts on the beauty of the Lord are framed, I suggest, within that bigger picture we've just outlined which is the headline story of the Bible from cover to cover. God's glory is that which identifies him as the ultimate in beauty. And the beauty of the Lord is the absolute standard by which all beauty is measured. How can we at this point have a real appreciation of it? We get some insight from the life of king David. David valued his place in God's house above everything else because he understood it to be the place from which to see the beauty of the Lord by means of seeking his face in worship there. This is what we read in Psalm 27:

> "One thing I have asked from the LORD, that I shall seek: That I may dwell in the house of the LORD all the days of my life, to behold the beauty of the LORD and to meditate in His temple ... Hear, O LORD, when I cry with my voice, and be gracious to me and answer me. When You said, "Seek My face," my heart said to You, "Your face, O LORD, I shall seek." Do not hide Your face from me ..." (Psalm 27:4-9).

This purpose for God's house is in fact the overarching purpose of God for all creation - inasmuch as, once sin is removed, his servants are to be able to see the beauty of his face in the eternal state described at the end of the book of Revelation (22:4). But how can we enjoy David's experience in this day and age? Where do we gaze upon the beauty of the Lord? Where is the biblical setting for worshipful meditations that might even exceed those David knew? For the answers to those questions, we need to begin our journey in the upper room where Jesus met with his disciples for the last time before his death, and to what's often referred to as the last supper. In Matthew's Gospel, we read in chapter 26:

> "While they were eating, Jesus took some bread, and after a blessing, He broke it and gave it to the disciples, and said, "Take, eat; this is My body." And when He had taken a cup and given thanks, He gave it to them, saying, "Drink from it, all of you; for this is My blood of the covenant, which is poured out for many for forgiveness of sins. "But I say to you, I will not drink of this fruit of the vine from now on until that day when I drink it new with you in My Father's kingdom" (Matthew 26:26-29).

The sequel to this is to be found in the New Testament Churches of God. As the Apostle Paul wrote to the Church of God at Corinth, in the first letter, eleventh chapter:

> "For I received from the Lord that which I also delivered to you, that the Lord Jesus in the night in which He was betrayed took bread; and when He had given thanks, He broke it and said, "This is My body, which is for you; do this in remembrance of Me." In the same way He took the cup also after supper, saying, "This cup is the new covenant in My blood; do this, as often as you drink it, in remembrance of Me." For as often as you eat this bread and drink the cup, you proclaim the Lord's death until He comes" (1 Corinthians 11:23-26).

"As often as you drink it," were the Lord's words. He never wants us to forget his passion. He's left us this memorial as a constant, a weekly, reminder. It was always on the first day of the week that the first disciples broke bread to remember the Lord (Acts 20:6,7) and the force of the words "as often as ..." imply that God's design is every week (see also 1 Corinthians 16:1,2). Whenever we gather as a church of God to sit around the Lord's table to eat the Lord's Supper, we have the most intimate and precious opportunity to meditate on what the Lord requires us to always remain mindful of.

As brothers lead God's people in worship, we find our hearts drawn to the Lord in all his true beauty. Isaiah the prophet wrote that at his first Advent, the Jews saw no beauty in him (Isaiah 53), but the Holy Spirit within present day worshippers enables us to enter into the experience of the hymn-writer who spoke of gathered worshipers: '... gazing on the Lord in glory ...' Another described our Lord, with his wounds described as being '... in beauty glorified.' In the beauty of holiness, as the psalmist once described Israel's worship experience - and we surely eclipse that as we focus on the glories of the Christ of God - in the beauty of holiness, we have a sense of spiritual awe as we "look upon the face of [God's] Anointed" (Psalm 84:9). There is no sight more beautiful than this. This will occupy and satisfy our minds for ever. "His servants shall see his face and do him service" (Revelation 22:4). Then God will be all in all. The whole earth full of his glory. There will be no distractions in a world to come that will be eternally free of sin. A paradise regained, and then some, where we will understand what true and absolute beauty is. And we shall be like him! An awareness of this as our destiny is surely what we should mostly be mindful of.

Through an appropriate mindfulness of our union with Christ through the cross, it's God's intention that moment by moment our lives become transformed to show a family resemblance to his son, Jesus. It's our destiny, after all, to be conformed to the image of God's son. Four words in Romans 8:30 stretch out like golden links in an eternal chain spanning from before time and away into the glorious for ever. These four words are the great theological words: chosen, called, justified and glorified. The last is also in the past tense, simply because it's one hundred percent certain, so it's as good as done. No believer can fall off this pathway which had its origin in the mists of eternity. All who were chosen will be glorified. These are the four most momentous words in our personal career! We're totally described by these four words in the most meaningful way. They sum up everything about our identity and destiny. And they have transforming power. Let's bask in an awareness and enjoyment of them that has the power to shape our every moment!

CHAPTER TWELVE: REVIEW QUESTIONS

1. Do you think it's correct to talk in terms of there being an absolute standard of beauty? If so, why? Otherwise, why not?
2. Where ideally should the David-style worshipful meditation on God's beauty find its place in our day? (Defend this biblically).
3. Which command of our Lord Jesus seems fundamental to mindfulness in terms of how it's a practical help to meditating regularly on our Lord's sacrifice?
4. A lot of books have been written on our selection, call and justification; less on our glorification. Try to outline what will be involved in the latter.

O PATIENT, SPOTLESS ONE!

O patient, spotless One!

Our hearts in meekness train,

To bear Thy yoke, and learn of Thee,

That we may rest obtain.

O Lord, Thou art enough

The mind and heart to fill;

Thy life to calm each anxious thought

Thy love each fear dispel.

O fix our earnest gaze

So wholly, Lord, on Thee,

That, with Thy beauty occupied,

We elsewhere none may see.

(Christian Andreas Bernstein)

SOME BIBLE VERSES TO MEMORISE

- Matthew 11:28-30: Come to me, all you who are weary and burdened, and I will give you rest. Take my yoke upon you and learn from me, for I am gentle and humble in heart, and you will find rest for your souls. For my yoke is easy and my burden is light.

- Romans 8:38-39: For I am convinced that neither death nor life, neither angels nor demons, neither the present nor the future, nor any powers, neither height nor depth, nor anything else in all creation, will be able to separate us from the love of God that is in Christ Jesus our Lord.

- Proverbs 3:5,6: Trust in the Lord with all your heart and lean not on your own understanding; in all your ways acknowledge him, and he will make your paths straight.

- Romans 12:1-2: Therefore, I urge you, brothers, in view of God's mercy, to offer your bodies as living sacrifices, holy and pleasing to God—this is your spiritual act of worship. Do not conform any longer to the pattern of this world, but be transformed by the renewing of your mind. Then you will be able to test and approve what God's will is—his good, pleasing and perfect will.

- Galatians 2:20: I have been crucified with Christ and I no longer live, but Christ lives in me. The life I live in the body, I live by faith in the Son of God, who loved me and gave himself for me.

- Ephesians 2:8,9: For it is by grace you have been saved, through faith—and this not from yourselves, it is the gift of God—not by works, so that no one can boast.

- 1 John 1:9: If we confess our sins, he is faithful and just and will forgive us our sins and purify us from all unrighteousness.

- Hebrews 12:1-2: Therefore, since we are surrounded by such a great cloud of witnesses, let us throw off everything that hinders and the sin that so easily entangles, and let us run with perseverance the race marked out for us. Let us fix our eyes on Jesus, the author and perfecter of our faith, who for the joy set before Him endured the cross, scorning its shame, and sat down at the right hand of the throne of God.

- Philippians 4:6,7: Do not be anxious about anything, but in everything, by prayer and petition, with thanksgiving, present your requests to God. And the peace of God, which transcends all understanding, will guard your hearts and your minds in Christ Jesus.

- 2 Corinthians 4:18: So we fix our eyes not on what is seen, but on what is unseen. For what is seen is temporary, but what is unseen is eternal.

SOME BIBLE PASSAGES TO MEDITATE ON

1. Isaiah 53
2. Psalm 23
3. 1 Corinthians 13
4. John 15
5. Psalm 139
6. Romans 8
7. Philippians 2
8. Psalm 1
9. Psalm 8
10. Revelation 1
11. 1 John 4:7-19
12. John 3:1-23

AN INTERVIEW WITH THE AUTHOR

Q: How did you come to write a book on Mindfulness?

A: Actually, I can't claim it was my own idea! It was suggested to me by my publisher that it would be a worthwhile topic to explore. To be completely honest, I was a little skeptical at first – partly as it wasn't a subject I was overly familiar with, and also what I'd heard about it raised some potential red flags about the Biblical basis for it. But, when I delved a bit deeper, I became gripped about the possibility of writing something that God might use to make a practical difference in the lives of Christians today.

Q: You've chosen a catchy title, some might say even slightly provocative – what was your thinking around that?

A: Well, the intention was to make people stop and think – quite appropriate, really! But seriously, as the book says, many people and organizations are giving "Mindfulness" their seal of approval - but are they endorsements Christians can trust? At the same time, a quick Google search will tell you that the concept of Mindfulness can be quite difficult to pin down. But, if we're able to go to the Bible for the definition, and also the 'how-to' guidance it gives, then we can be quite comfortable we're talking about something that Jesus would be happy with, even if "Mindfulness" wasn't such a buzz word then as it seems to be now!

Q: So you're saying that Mindfulness is actually a Bible concept?

A: The specific word is never used, of course, but the word 'mindful' does crop up and the concept appears in many forms when we start looking for it. There's nothing new about things like meditation, which was something that David practised way back in the Old Testament – but the Bible version has two key twists that make all the difference. Today's

Mindfulness tends to be inward-looking, and one of its goals is to clear the mind. For the Christian, it's the exact opposite – it's all about looking outward to God, and filling our mind with a sense of His presence, power and purposes.

Q. What comes across in the book is that your convinced that the mind is absolutely key to the Christian life – is that fair?

A: Very much so. Psychologists have long known how powerful the mind is, although sadly some of them might attribute it to random, meaningless evolutionary processes. As Christians, we know differently – that it's designed by an all-powerful Creator. But perhaps we haven't fully appreciated just what it can do in terms of driving our discipleship. The Christian experience begins with something the Bible calls 'repentance' which is essentially a change of mind. The Apostle Paul goes on to characterize Christianity to Timothy (2 Tim.1:7) in terms of power, love and a sound mind. It's clear God intends that the reasonable truths of Biblical Christianity should first engage our mind before settling deep into our heart ... the ultimate goal being that we arrive at the mind of Christ.

Q: You don't spend a lot of time in the book exploring what might be called "secular mindfulness" – was that deliberate?

A: Yes, it was. I've been impressed by what Tim Challies has to say in his book on spiritual discernment about focusing on the truth. He points out that bank clerks aren't trained to spot counterfeit currency by studying fakes – they invest their time scrutinizing the real thing so that the fakes become immediately obvious! So the book really sketches out the 'Oprah Winfrey' version in thumbnail only, so we can focus on what really matters – what the Bible has to teach us – so that anything else we encounter will seem inferior by comparison.

Q: At the last count, you've written 60 books on prophecy, discipleship, apologetics, you name it – how do you manage to be both so prolific and varied?

A: I don't really keep score but, in my defence, many of them are quite short! The secret is that I teach on a weekly radio podcast called Search For Truth, which has had a real mix of content over the years. It requires a disciplined writing schedule, but the scripts for these programmes provide ready material for books; of course, it's the other way around with this one – as the research for it resulted in an upcoming podcast series. Another imminent series is entitled "Amazing Grace - Paul's Gospel Message to the Galatians", so look out for the accompanying book – it sounds like it's number 61!

MORE TITLES FROM THE AUTHOR

DANIEL DECODED: DECIPHERING BIBLE PROPHECY

The book of Daniel is perhaps the most half-read in all the Bible! The first half is full of well-loved Sunday School stories and the second contains complex prophecies about the end times. Brian Johnston explores both halves in this engaging study, which is sure to get you thinking – about both the present and the future!

IF ATHEISM IS TRUE: THE FUTILE FAITH AND HOPELESS HYPOTHESES OF DAWKINS & CO.

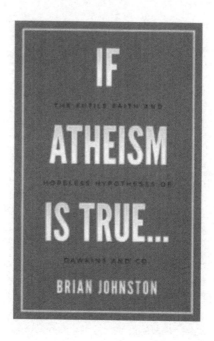

This book draws together some of the author's previously published writings on apologetics to produce a concerted offensive against what the apostle Paul would surely describe as the 'indefensible' arguments of the so-called 'New Atheists'. The short chapters in Brian's conversational style serve as an ideal entry-level primer for anyone wanting to get to grips with one of the most important of today's debates.

AMAZING GRACE! PAUL'S GOSPEL MESSAGE TO THE GALATIANS

Paul had a blunt message for the Galatians - we aren't saved as a result of what we might do to please God, because Jesus already pleased him at the cross! Now what God wants from us is grace-based obedience, not performance-based legalism. Perhaps that's a message we all still need to hear...

Also by Brian Johnston

Healthy Churches - God's Bible Blueprint For Growth
Hope for Humanity: God's Fix for a Broken World
First Corinthians: Nothing But Christ Crucified
Bible Answers to Listeners' Questions
Living in God's House: His Design in Action
Christianity 101: Seven Bible Basics
Nights of Old: Bible Stories of God at Work
Daniel Decoded: Deciphering Bible Prophecy
A Test of Commitment: 15 Challenges to Stimulate Your Devotion to
Christ
John's Epistles - Certainty in the Face of Change
If Atheism Is True...
Brian Johnston Box Set 1
8 Amazing Privileges of God's People: A Bible Study of Romans 9:4-5
Learning from Bible Grandparents
Increasing Your Christian Footprint
Christ-centred Faith
Mindfulness That Jesus Endorses
Amazing Grace! Paul's Gospel Message to the Galatians
Abraham: Friend of God

About the Author

Born and educated in Scotland, Brian worked as a government scientist until God called him into full-time Christian ministry on behalf of the Churches of God (www.churchesofgod.info). His voice has been heard on Search For Truth radio broadcasts for over 30 years during which time he has been an itinerant Bible teacher throughout the UK and Canada. His evangelical and missionary work outside the UK is primarily in Belgium and The Philippines. He is married to Rosemary, with a son and daughter.

About the Publisher

Hayes Press (www.hayespress.org) is a registered charity in the United Kingdom, whose primary mission is to disseminate the Word of God, mainly through literature. It is one of the largest distributors of gospel tracts and leaflets in the United Kingdom, with over 100 titles and hundreds of thousands despatched annually.

Hayes Press also publishes Plus Eagles Wings, a fun and educational Bible magazine for children, and Golden Bells, a popular daily Bible reading calendar in wall or desk formats.

Also available are over 100 Bibles in many different versions, shapes and sizes, Christmas cards, Christian jewellery, Eikos Bible Art, Bible text posters and much more!